What Every Teacher Should Know About No Child Left Behind

Nathan L. Essex
Southwest Tennessee Community College
and
University of Memphis

Boston   New York   San Francisco
Mexico City   Montreal   Toronto   London   Madrid   Munich   Paris
Hong Kong   Singapore   Tokyo   Cape Town   Sydney

Copyright © 2006 Pearson Education, Inc.

All rights reserved. No part of the material protected by this copyright notice may be reproduced or utilized in any form or by any means, electronic or mechanical, including photocopying, recording, or by any information storage and retrieval system, without written permission from the copyright owner.

To obtain permission(s) to use material from this work, please submit a written request to Allyn and Bacon, Permissions Department, 75 Arlington Street, Boston, MA 02116, or fax your request to 617-848-7320.

Between the time website information is gathered and then published, it is not unusual for some sites to have closed. Also, the transcription of URLs can result in typographical errors. The publisher would appreciate notification where these errors occur so that they may be corrected in subsequent editions.

ISBN 0-205-48256-2

Printed in the United States of America

10 9 8 7 6 5 4 3 2   09 08 07 06

Contents

Chapter 1   What Is No Child Left Behind?   1

The No Child Left Behind Act—
    Basic Provisions   1
    Reduced Bureaucracy and Increased
        Flexibility   2
    Increased Accountability for Student
        Performance   3
    Parental Empowerment   3
Summary of Key Requirements of NCLB   4
    Adequate Yearly Progress   4
    Public School Choice   4
    Supplemental Services   4
    Unsafe School Choice Option (USCO)   5
    Exceptional Students   5
    School Improvement   5
    Limited English Proficiency Students   5
    Assessments   5
    Participation in State NAEP   7
    Stronger Accountability for Results   7
    Increased Freedom for States and
        Communities   7
    Proven Education Methods   8
    More Choices for Parents   8
    The Importance of No Child Left
        Behind to America   8

Chapter 2   How Does NCLB Apply to Schools?   10

Schools in Need of Improvement   10
How Does NCLB Apply to Teachers?   11
The Impact on Teachers   11
What Does "Highly Qualified" Mean
    for Teachers?   12
    Teacher Qualifications   13
    Qualifications for Teachers and
        Paraprofessionals   13
Improving Teaching and Learning   14
Teachers' Knowledge of Subject Matter   15
    New Elementary School Teachers   15
    New Middle and High School Teachers   15
    Experienced Elementary, Middle School,
        and High School Teachers   16

Teacher Testing	16
Information and Assistance by the Federal Government Teacher Assistance Corps	18
Teacher-Quality Web Site	18
Teacher-to-Teacher Summer Workshops	18
Research-to-Practice Summit	18
Funding for Teacher Quality	19
Improving the Academic Achievement of the Disadvantaged (Title I)	19
Improving Teacher-Quality State Grants (Title II)	19
District Needs Assessment	20
Educational Technology State Grants Program (Title II)	20
English Language Acquisition State Grants Program (Title III)	20
Other Programs to Improve Teaching and Learning	21
Report Cards and Parent Notification	21
Report Cards	21
National Board Certification	23
Advanced Certification/Advanced Credentialing	23
How Does NCLB Apply to Students?	25
Student Improvement	25
Accountability for Student Performance	26
School Dropout Prevention	30
Performance Measurement	31
Improving Academic Achievement of Disadvantaged Students	31
Key Requirements	32
Performance Measurement	33
Accountability for Student Programs	33
Key Requirements	34
Performance Measurement	34
Improving Math and Science Instruction Around the Nation	35
Student Performance in 2003	37
Math and Science Partnerships	37
Teacher Liability Protection	38

Women's Educational Equity		40
Performance Measurement		41
Enhancing Education through		
Technology		41
Key Requirements		42
Performance Measurement		43

Chapter 3   **Parental Empowerment and**
Innovative Programs   **44**

Expanded Parental Options	44
Important Information for Parents on	
Student Performance	44
New Options to Parents Whose Children	
Attend Schools in Need of	
Improvement	44
Expanded Flexibility and Local Control	45
More Flexible Spending	45
Parents' Right to Know	45
Parent Notification	46
Parental Assistance Information Centers	46
Provisions Related to Parental Assistance	47
Reduced Bureaucracy and Increased	
Flexibility	47
Focused Academic Standards	47
Key Requirements	47
Voluntary Public School Choice	49
New Features of The No Child Left	
Behind Act: Improved Accountability	
for Student Performance	49
Parental Empowerment	49
Key Requirements	50
Performance Measurement	50
Key Activities Involving State Education	
Agencies	51
Magnet Schools Assistance	51
Added Features of the No Child Left	
Behind Act	51
Reduced Bureaucracy and Increased	
Flexibility	52
Increased Funds for Planning	52
Key Requirements	25

v

Partnerships in Character Education	53
What's New—The No Child Left Behind Act	53
Reduced Bureaucracy and Increased Flexibility	54
The Act Eliminates Requirements for State Clearinghouses	54
Key Requirements	54
Performance Measurement	55
Key Activities Involving State Education Agencies	55
Star Schools	55
Key Requirements	56
Ready to Teach	56
Key Requirements	57
Performance Measurement	58
What's New—The No Child Left Behind Act	58
Gun-Free Requirements	59
Other Major Program Changes	60
Questions Teachers Frequently Ask about No Child Left Behind	61
Highly Qualified Teacher Requirements	61
Accountability	73
Student Assessment	76
Students with Disabilities	77
Reading	78
Scientifically Based Research	79
Safe Schools	80
Learning More About No Child Left Behind: Unanswered Questions Regarding No Child Left Behind	81
Dispelling the Myths of No Child Left Behind	81
Emerging Legal Issues Involving No Child Left Behind	84
References	**85**
Index	**87**

Chapter 1

What Is No Child Left Behind?

The No Child Left Behind Act of 2001 (NCLB) is a landmark educational reform initiative designed to improve student achievement and change the culture of schools in America. NCLB raises expectations for all states, local school systems, and schools in terms of ensuring that all students meet or exceed state standards in reading and mathematics within their twelve years of schooling. NCLB requires all states to establish state academic standards and a state testing system that meet federal requirements. NCLB passed with overwhelming bipartisan support from Congress, and was signed into law by President George W. Bush on January 8, 2002.

With passage of No Child Left Behind, Congress reauthorized the Elementary and Secondary Education Act of 1965 (ESEA)—the principal federal law affecting education from kindergarten through high school. In amending ESEA, the new law represents a sweeping overhaul of federal efforts to support elementary and secondary education in the United States. It is built on four common-sense pillars: **accountability for results, an emphasis on doing what works based on scientific research, expanded parental options,** and **expanded local control and flexibility.**

The No Child Left Behind Act—Basic Provisions

- **Requires that Title I funds be used only for effective educational practices.** Title I schoolwide and targeted assistance programs are required to use effective methods and instructional strategies that are grounded in scientifically based research. School improvement plans, professional development activities, and technical assistance that districts provide to low-performing schools must be based on strategies that have a proven record of effectiveness.
- **Requires states to develop plans with annual measurable objectives that will ensure that all teachers teaching in**

1

core academic subjects are highly qualified by the end of the 2005–06 school year.

- **Requires local school districts to ensure that all Title I teachers in core academic subjects hired after the first day of the 2002–03 school year are "highly qualified."** For new teachers, this means being certified by the state (including alternative routes to state certification), holding at least a bachelor's degree, and demonstrating subject area competency.
- **Strengthens corrective action** (required after two years of school improvement) to include actions more likely to bring about meaningful change at the school, such as replacing school staff responsible for the continued failure to make adequate yearly progress, implementing a new curriculum, and reorganizing the school internally.
- **Mandates the fundamental restructuring of any school that fails to improve over an extended period of time.** Restructuring may include reopening the school as a charter school or turning over school operations either to the state or to a private company with a demonstrated record of effectiveness.
- **Strengthens paraprofessional requirements.** Stronger standards include two years of postsecondary education or, for an applicant with a high school diploma, the demonstration of necessary skills on a formal state or local academic assessment. All new hires must meet these requirements, and existing paraprofessionals have four years to comply with them.
- Emphasizes that paraprofessionals may not provide instructional support services. Paraprofessionals may not offer instruction except under the direct supervision of a teacher.

Reduced Bureaucracy and Increased Flexibility

- **NCLB expands eligibility for schoolwide programs.** The poverty threshold for schoolwide programs, which enable schools to use Title I funds to raise the achievement of at-risk students by improving the quality of instruction throughout the school, has been lowered from 50 percent to 40 percent.

Increased Accountability for Student Performance

- **The Act requires annual assessments in grades 3–8** that include all students.
- **Requires state and local report cards** on student academic achievement.
- **Requires states to implement a single statewide accountability system.**
- **Tightens provisions concerning adequate yearly progress** by requiring states to specify annual measurable objectives to assess student progress to ensure that all groups of students—disaggregated by poverty, race and ethnicity, disability, and limited English proficiency data—reach proficiency in reading and math within 12 years.
- **Substantially increases funding for state and local support for school improvement.** Increased funding rose (from one-half percent of Title I funds under the 1994 Elementary and Secondary Education Act reauthorization to two percent under the No Child Left Behind Act, rising to four percent in 2004). Also establishes a separate $500 million authorization for Assistance for Local School Improvement grants.

Parental Empowerment

- **The Act requires local school districts to offer public school choice to students in schools identified for improvement, corrective action, or restructuring.** This provision ensures that no student is trapped in an under-performing school. School districts must provide transportation for eligible students, subject to the 20 percent rule described below.
- **Requires school districts to permit low-income students attending chronically under-performing schools to obtain supplemental educational services from a public- or private-sector provider.** Providers must have been approved by the state. Faith-based organizations are eligible to apply for approval to provide supplemental educational services.
- **Requires school districts to spend an amount equal to 20 percent of their Part A funds for transportation of students who exercise a choice option or for supplemen-**

tal educational services. This amount is required unless a lesser amount is needed to meet all requests. These funds may not necessarily be taken from Title I allocations, but may be provided from other allowable federal, state, local or private sources.

- **Notifies parents of school choice and supplemental educational services options.** This provision requires districts to "promptly" notify parents of eligible students attending schools identified for improvement, corrective action, or restructuring of their option to transfer their child to a better public school or to obtain supplemental educational services.
- **Establishes parents' "Right to Know" provision.** This provision requires local school districts to annually notify parents of their right to request information on the professional qualifications of their children's teachers.

Summary of Key Requirements of NCLB

Adequate Yearly Progress

Adequate Yearly Progress (AYP) is one of the cornerstones of the federal No Child Left Behind (NCLB) Act. It is a measure of year-to-year student achievement on statewide assessments.

Public School Choice

Under No Child Left Behind, children who attend public schools that have not made Adequate Yearly Progress (AYP) for two or more consecutive years and have thus been designated for Needs Improvement have the option of moving to a higher performing public school.

Supplemental Services

Under the No Child Left Behind Act, children in schools that have been in Needs Improvement status for two or more years may receive supplemental services that include before- and after-school tutoring or remedial classes in reading, language arts, and math.

Unsafe School Choice Option (USCO)

Under No Child Left Behind, states must develop a definition of "persistently dangerous" schools and allow public school choice for students who have been victims of a violent criminal offense or who attend a school that meets the definition.

Exceptional Students

Ensuring that no student with disabilities is left behind under No Child Left Behind, all students, including students with disabilities, must meet Georgia's proficient level of academic achievement by 2013–2014.

School Improvement

Schools are required to design and implement an effective system of support to enhance school improvement with an intense focus on schools that fail to make adequate yearly progress.

Limited English Proficiency Students

Under No Child Left Behind, all students, including students with limited English proficiency (LEP), must meet their state's proficiency level of academic achievement by 2013–2014. LEP students will become proficient in English and reach high academic standards, at a minimum attaining proficiency or better in reading/language arts and mathematics.

The No Child Left Behind Act strengthens Title I requirements for state assessments, accountability systems, and support for school improvement. The law also establishes minimum qualifications for teachers and paraprofessionals in Title I programs.

Assessments

By the 2005–06 school year, states must develop and implement annual assessments in reading and mathematics in grades 3 through 8 and at least once in grades 10–12. By

2007–08, states also must administer annual science assessments at least once in grades 3–5, grades 6–9, and grades 10–12. These assessments must be aligned with state academic content and achievement standards and involve multiple measures, including measures of higher-order thinking and understanding.

- **Alignment with State Standards.** State assessments must be aligned with challenging academic content standards and challenging academic achievement standards. States were required under the previous law to develop or adopt standards in mathematics and reading/language arts, and the new law requires the development of science standards by 2005 and 2006. Their standards require that all students meet the same expectations including at least three achievement levels.
- **Inclusion.** State assessments must provide for the participation of all students, including students with disabilities or limited English proficiency. Students enrolled in schools in the United States for three consecutive years must be assessed in English in the area of reading and language arts.
- **Accommodations.** State assessments must provide for reasonable accommodations for students with disabilities or limited English proficiency, including, if practicable, native-language versions of the assessment.
- **Annual Assessment of English Proficiency.** Beginning with the 2002–03 school year, states are required to ensure that districts administer tests of English proficiency—that measure oral language, reading, and writing skills in English—to all limited English proficient students.
- **Reporting.** State assessment systems must produce results disaggregated by gender, major racial and ethnic groups, English proficiency, migrant status, disability, and status as economically advantaged. The assessment system must produce individual student interpretive, descriptive, and diagnostic reports. States must report itemized score analyses to districts and schools.
- **Prompt Dissemination of Results.** States must ensure that the results of state assessments administered in one school year are available to school districts before the beginning of

the next school year. The assessment results must be provided in a manner that is clear and easy to understand and be used by school districts, schools and teachers to improve the educational achievement of individual students.

Participation in State NAEP

States must participate in biennial National Assessment of Educational Progress (NAEP) assessments in reading and mathematics for fourth- and eighth-graders, beginning in 2002–03. State-level NAEP data will enable policymakers to examine the relative rigor of state standards and assessments against a common metric.

Stronger Accountability for Results

Under No Child Left Behind, states are working to close the achievement gap and ensure that all students, including those who are disadvantaged, achieve academic proficiency. Annual state and school district report cards inform parents and communities of state and school progress. Schools that do not make progress must provide supplemental services, such as free tutoring or after-school assistance; take corrective actions; and, if still not making adequate yearly progress after five years, make dramatic changes to the way the school is run.

Increased Freedom for States and Communities

Under No Child Left Behind, states and school districts have unprecedented flexibility in how they use federal education funds. For example, it is possible for most school districts to transfer up to 50 percent of the federal formula grant funds they receive under the Improving Teacher Quality State Grants, Educational Technology, Innovative Programs, and Safe and Drug-Free Schools programs to any one of these programs, or to their Title I program, without separate approval. This flexibility allows districts to use funds for their particular needs, such as hiring new teachers, increasing teacher pay, and improving teacher training and professional development.

Proven Education Methods

No Child Left Behind places emphasis on determining which educational programs and practices have been proven effective through rigorous scientific research. Federal funding is targeted to support these programs and teaching methods that work to improve student learning and achievement. In reading, for example, No Child Left Behind supports scientifically based instruction programs in the early grades under the Reading First program and in preschool under the Early Reading First program.

More Choices for Parents

Parents of children in low-performing schools are provided new options under No Child Left Behind. In schools that do not meet state standards for at least two consecutive years, parents may transfer their children to a better-performing public school, including a public charter school, within their district. The district must provide transportation, using Title I funds if necessary. Students from low-income families in schools that fail to meet state standards for at least three years are eligible to receive supplemental educational services, including tutoring, after-school services, and summer school. Also, students who attend a persistently dangerous school or are the victim of a violent crime while in their school have the option to attend a safe school within their district.

The Importance of No Child Left Behind to America

Despite decades of hard work and dedication to education in America, achievement gaps remain noticeably wide. Since 1965, when the Elementary and Secondary Education Act (ESEA) was enacted in Congress, the federal government has spent more than $267.4 billion to assist states in educating disadvantaged children. Yet, according to the most recent National Assessment of Educational Progress (NAEP) on reading in 2002, only 31 percent of fourth-graders can read at a proficient (passing) or advanced level. Achievement among the highest-performing students remained stable, and America's lowest performers have improved only slightly.

On a positive note, many schools across the country have improved academic achievement for children with a history of low performance. Teachers and administrators are working collectively in schools to target areas of weakness, improve skills and spend money more wisely, producing better results for all children.

While spending increased in the 1980s and 1990s, achievement remained flat. Clearly, resources and effort are not lacking as educators around the nation work to improve student achievement. The reauthorized Elementary and Secondary Education Act, called No Child Left Behind, calls for states, districts and schools to be accountable for dollars spent on education. NCLB creates a culture of accountability, requiring schools to reassess what they are doing to raise achievement of all students and support teaching and learning.

Chapter 2

How Does NCLB Apply to Schools?

NCLB does not label any school as "failing." In fact, states are responsible for identifying schools as "in need of improvement" if they do not reach the state-defined standards for two consecutive years. Far from losing federal funds, schools in need of improvement actually qualify for additional support to assist them in getting back on track. Federal funds have steadily increased to support schools in need of improvement. These schools increased funding targeted for professional development and are specifically required to work with parents, school staff, district, and outside experts to develop an improvement plan. The regular assessments that NCLB sanctions help schools identify subject areas and teaching methods that need improvement. For example, if student reading scores do not reach the state's benchmark for two consecutive years, the school knows it needs to improve its reading program. In the past, these schools might not have received the attention and support needed to improve. Through No Child Left Behind, every state has made a commitment that it will no longer turn a blind eye when schools are not meeting the needs of **every** student in their care.

Schools in Need of Improvement

NCLB provides schools with assistance when a school is "in need of improvement." School officials are required to collaborate with parents, school staff, district leaders and outside experts to develop a plan to improve the school. The district must ensure that the school receives needed technical assistance as it develops and implements its improvement plan. Examples of technical assistance include:

- Identifying problems in instruction or curriculum.
- Analyzing and revising the school's budget so that resources are more effectively targeted to activities most likely to facilitate student learning.

The school's improvement plan must implement strategies, relying on scientifically based research that will strengthen mastery of core academic subjects, especially the subject areas that resulted in the school being deemed in need of improvement. **Schools in need of improvement must spend at least ten percent of their Title I funds to assist teachers.** For example, they may provide professional development that will improve subject-matter knowledge in the subjects taught. These schools also are expected to develop strategies to promote effective parental involvement in the school and to incorporate a teacher-mentoring program. No Child Left Behind provides several additional funding sources that schools can use to support teachers and assist them in improving their skills.

How Does NCLB Apply to Teachers?

No Child Left Behind outlines the minimum qualifications needed by teachers: a bachelor's degree, full state certification, and demonstration of subject-matter competency for each subject taught. NCLB requires that states develop plans to achieve the goal that all teachers of core academic subjects are highly qualified by the end of the 2005–06 school year. States must include in their plans annual, measurable objectives that each local school district and school must meet in moving toward the goal. They must also report their progress on annual report cards.

The Impact on Teachers

Student test results will affect everyone employed by the school district. **K–3 teachers** must teach all children to read. These teachers must learn how to assess children and how to use assessment results to plan effective instruction. If a child is not making progress with one method of instruction, the teacher must use a different, more appropriate method. Teachers must use research-based methods of teaching and be knowledgeable regarding phonemic awareness and phonics, even though they may not have been exposed to research based on teaching methods in their preparation programs.

Many teacher-training programs do not require students to acquire knowledge regarding research-based teaching methods or phonemes in order to graduate. Many states do not require this knowledge for certification or licensure of elementary school teachers. Under the No Child Left Behind Act, elementary school teachers must meet the new "highly qualified" standard.

Teachers who teach upper elementary grades must teach math, reading, and science at higher skill levels. These teachers must possess the skills to teach many levels of students. Annual testing will indicate the amount of gain made by students regarding individual teachers. Schools will not be able to retain ineffective teachers. The stakes are simply too high.

Middle school and high school teachers must meet the new "highly qualified" standard in the subjects they teach. Teachers in higher grades are responsible for gains made by their students. These teachers will be responsible for educating students who transfer into their schools without the level of instruction they should have received.

Music teachers, gym teachers, computer teachers, and foreign language teachers are not immune from this law. If their school must offer school choice, many of their students may leave. It may be necessary that they follow the students to a better school and teach the rising population there.

Speech pathologists, occupational therapists, physical therapists and guidance counselors may be required to integrate academics into their therapies to compensate for the child's time out of the classroom. When children exercise their school choice options and leave unsuccessful schools, there may not be a need for as many related service providers.

Special education teachers must teach students to the appropriate level of proficiency. If a special education teacher teaches a core subject, he/she must meet the standard of a highly qualified teacher in that subject. Special education teachers must work more closely with regular educators. A student may take an alternative assessment if his/her disabilities prevent him/her from taking the regular state assessment but alternative assessments must test grade level knowledge.

What Does "Highly Qualified" Mean for Teachers?

There is considerable confusion regarding what No Child Left Behind's highly qualified teacher provisions include and what they mean for individual teachers.

Teacher Qualifications

Recent studies offer compelling evidence that teachers are one of the most critical factors in how well students achieve. For instance, studies in both Tennessee and Texas found that students who had effective teachers greatly outperformed those who had ineffective teachers. In the Tennessee study, students with highly effective teachers for three consecutive years scored 50 percentage points higher on a test of math skills than those whose teachers were ineffective.

As stated previously, No Child Left Behind includes provisions stating that all teachers in core academic areas must be highly qualified in the core academic subjects they teach by the end of the 2005–06 school year. It also requires that newly hired teachers in Title I programs or schools be highly qualified immediately. A more flexible timeline is allowed for teachers in eligible small, rural schools, who often teach multiple subjects.

All teachers hired after the first day of the 2002–03 school year in Title I school-wide programs must be highly qualified. However, in Title I targeted-assistance schools, only those teachers paid with Title I funds need to be highly qualified immediately. Teachers should check with their district to determine their school designation.

"Highly qualified" is a specific term defined by No Child Left Behind. The law outlines a list of minimum requirements related to content knowledge and teaching skills that a highly qualified teacher would meet. The law, however, also recognizes the importance of state and local control of education and therefore provides the opportunity for each state to develop a definition of highly qualified that is consistent with NCLB as well as with the unique needs of the state.

Qualifications for Teachers and Paraprofessionals

The No Child Left Behind Act requires states to ensure that Title I schools provide instruction by highly qualified instructional staff.

- **Highly Qualified Teachers.** States must develop plans with annual measurable objectives that will ensure that all teachers of core academic subjects are highly qualified, which

13

again means that they have state certification (which may be alternative state certification), hold a bachelor's degree, and have demonstrated subject area competency. Core academic subjects include English, reading or language arts, mathematics, science, foreign languages, civics and government, economics, arts, history, and geography. All new hires in Title I programs after the start of the 2002–03 school year must meet these requirements; all existing teachers must meet these requirements by the end of the 2005–06 school year. School districts must use at least five percent of their Title I funds for professional development to assist teachers in becoming highly qualified.

- **Higher Qualifications for Paraprofessionals.** Paraprofessionals in Title I programs must have at least two years of postsecondary education or, for an applicant with a high school diploma, demonstrate necessary skills on a formal state or local academic assessment. All new hires in Title I programs after January 8, 2002, must meet these requirements; existing paraprofessionals have four years from January 8, 2002, to comply with these requirements. However, these requirements do not apply to paraprofessionals used for translation or parent involvement. All paraprofessionals in Title I programs must have earned a high school diploma or its equivalent.

- **Appropriate Roles for Paraprofessionals.** The law specifies that paraprofessionals may not provide instructional support services except under the direct supervision of a teacher.

Improving Teaching and Learning

States have the flexibility to create high-quality assessments, aligned with state standards for schools with a focus on higher-level thinking skills. Districts and schools may use these assessments to measure progress in student learning. These annual tests provide educators with information regarding each child's academic strengths and weaknesses. With this knowledge, teachers can craft lessons to ensure that each student meets or exceeds the standards. In addition, principals may use these data to assess where the school should invest resources. For example, tests may reveal that students are doing well with respect to multiplication but are experiencing difficulty with fractions. This assessment data might mean that the curriculum for teaching fractions needs to be adjusted or that teachers need additional professional development in teaching fractions.

NCLB requires that all teachers demonstrate competency in the subjects they are assigned to teach. Schools must document that all enrolled students have highly qualified teachers in their classrooms who are competent in the subjects they teach. Competency may be demonstrated by (a) passing a subject matter test or (b) earning credit hours that are equivalent to a degree in the subject areas they teach.

Under high, objective, uniform state standards of evaluation, states are provided the flexibility to develop their own standards that apply to current teachers as a means of demonstrating subject matter competency in their assigned subjects. Teachers may earn points through a combination of teaching experience, professional development activities and demonstrated knowledge that has been gained over a period of time. Points also may be earned through service to the community in which the teacher's school serves.

Teachers' Knowledge of Subject Matter

Students, parents, and educators intuitively believe that a teacher's knowledge of subject matter is critical if students are expected to achieve high standards. Having teachers who are well versed in the content they are teaching is good practice because it leads to improved student learning.

New Elementary School Teachers

Elementary school teachers who are new to the profession must demonstrate competency by passing a rigorous state test on subject knowledge and teaching skills in reading and language arts, writing, math, and other areas of the basic elementary school curriculum.

New Middle and High School Teachers

At the middle and high school levels, new teachers must demonstrate competency either by passing a rigorous state test in

15

each subject they teach or by completing an academic major or coursework equivalent to an academic major, an advanced degree or advanced certification or credentials.

Experienced Elementary, Middle School, and High School Teachers

Teachers with experience must either meet the requirements for new teachers or demonstrate competency based on a system designed by each state. No Child Left Behind recognizes that many teachers who have experience may currently possess qualifications necessary to be considered highly qualified. Therefore, the law allows states to create a high, objective, uniform state standard of evaluation (HOUSSE). This standard is defined by each state in line with six basic criteria established in NCLB. HOUSSE allows states to evaluate teachers' subject matter knowledge by recognizing, among other things, their teaching experience, professional development and knowledge in the subject garnered over time in the profession. Requirements for uniform state standards are identified in Table 2.1.

This evaluation may involve multiple, objective measures of teacher competency. Most states have developed their high, objective, uniform state standards of evaluation (HOUSSE) standards for experienced teachers. Many are using point systems that allow teachers to count a combination of years of successful classroom experience, participation in high-quality professional development that evaluates what the teacher has learned, service on curriculum-development teams and other important activities related to the development of content-area expertise. As states begin implementing these standards, many experienced teachers may find that they already meet the competency requirements for the subjects they teach. Others may need to take only minimal steps to meet the requirements. Teachers should contact their state department of education regarding the status of their state's HOUSSE provision for experienced teachers.

Teacher Testing

Under No Child Left Behind, it is **not** mandatory for all teachers to take a test to determine that they meet their state's

TABLE 2.1 • *High, Objective, Uniform State Standard of Evaluation (HOUSSE) Standards*

The law requires that such standards:

- Are set by the state for grade-appropriate academic subject-matter knowledge and teaching skills.

- Are aligned with challenging state academic content standards and student achievement standards and developed in consultation with core content specialists, teachers, principals, and school administrators.

- Provide objective, coherent information about the teacher's attainment of core content knowledge in the academic subjects in which a teacher teaches.

- Are applied uniformly to all teachers in the same academic subject and the same grade level throughout the state.

- Take into consideration, but are not based primarily on, the time a teacher has been teaching the academic subject.

- Are made available to the public upon request.

Source: No Child Left Behind Act.

---

highly qualified teacher requirements in the subjects they teach. Testing is required only for new elementary teachers. States have the flexibility to create and make determinations regarding subject-matter tests for teachers, and NCLB allows new and experienced secondary teachers to demonstrate competency through a major or its equivalent in the subject, or through an advanced degree or certification. As each state defines its own grade-level content standards, it may choose appropriate assessments for new teachers and provide opportunities for experienced teachers to demonstrate subject-matter knowledge through a test or other means.

17

Information and Assistance by the Federal Government Teacher Assistance Corps

At the direction of former Secretary Rod Paige, the U.S. Department of Education formed the Teacher Assistance Corps (TAC), to assist states in implementing the highly qualified teacher requirements in the law. Consisting of practitioners, state and district officials, researchers, higher education leaders and others, TAC teams have provided assistance in understanding the law, shared innovative practices from other states, and visited states as they shared implementation challenges. Many states invited principals, superintendents, and teachers to these meetings, allowing them an opportunity to raise questions and voice concerns. The TAC initiative will provide further assistance, as needed, while states are in the process of all phases of implementation.

Teacher-Quality Web Site

The U.S. Department of Education sponsors the Web site **www.teacherquality.us.** It includes links to information on many interesting state and district initiatives across the nation focused on improving teaching and learning, along with other information specifically designed for classroom teachers.

Teacher-to-Teacher Summer Workshops

The U.S. Department of Education has assembled some of the nation's most effective teachers and education experts to share with their colleagues research-based practices and effective methods of using data to improve instruction.

Research-to-Practice Summit

The U.S. Department of Education will sponsor a Research-to-Practice Summit, where the latest findings of effective teaching and learning will be presented. Teacher practitioners will share how they have applied those findings in everyday teaching and how they have equipped their students to reach unprecedented levels of success.

Teachers may register to receive electronic updates from the Department. These short e-bytes address some of the hot topics from the department's teacher outreach and provide links to resources to aid teachers in acquiring information regarding the latest policy, research, and professional issues affecting the classroom. Teachers may register at: **www.teacherquality.us.**

Funding for Teacher Quality

No Child Left Behind provides funds to states and districts to conduct a wide variety of activities aimed at supporting teachers. It is important to note that districts can transfer up to 50 percent of federal formula grant funds they receive under different parts of the law (Title II—Improving Teacher Quality and Educational Technology, Title IV—Safe and Drug-Free School Grants, Title V—Innovative Programs) to any one of these programs or to their Title I program (Improving the Academic Achievement of the Disadvantaged). This provision allows districts to target resources as they see fit, including moving funds into Title II to provide even more support for teachers. This provision can be accomplished without separate requests and approval.

Improving the Academic Achievement of the Disadvantaged (Title I)

Each district that receives Title I funds must spend at least five percent of its Title I allocation on professional development activities to assist teachers. In fiscal year (FY) 2004, Title I funding included about $605.2 million targeted to professional development alone. With a record request of $13.3 billion for the program in FY 2005, the amount targeted to professional development would minimally be $653.7 million.

Improving Teacher-Quality State Grants (Title II)

No Child Left Behind makes funds available specifically to assist all states, support teachers, and improve teaching and learning. Funding for FY 2004 was $2.93 billion; total funding from FY 2002-04 amounts to more than $8.7 billion. States have, in fact, submitted applications to the Department describ-

19

ing their annual goals for increasing the percentage of highly qualified teachers. States also have described how they will use funds to meet the teacher and paraprofessional requirements of the law and how they will hold districts accountable for their progress in assisting all teachers to reach the highly qualified standard for the subjects they teach.

District Needs Assessment

To receive Title II funds, each district must conduct a needs assessment outlining activities that must be implemented to provide teachers with the content knowledge and teaching skills they need and to provide principals the instructional leadership skills they need to assist teachers. No Child Left Behind requires that teachers participate in the needs assessment process. **Teachers should contact their state or district regarding their involvement in this process, if they have not already been invited to participate.**

Educational Technology State Grants Program (Title II)

Each district receiving Educational Technology State Grants funds must spend at least 25 percent (a total of $173 million in FY 2004) on high-quality professional development in the integration of technology into curricula and instruction, unless a district can demonstrate that it currently provides such training.

English Language Acquisition State Grants Program (Title III)

In FY 2004, $548 million is available to states for English Language Acquisition State Grants under Title III of NCLB. States may use up to five percent of these funds for professional development and other uses to support teachers. In addition, more than $68 million dollars is available specifically for professional development projects to assist districts and schools in improving the teaching of English language learners. Of this amount, $39 million is available for project-grants under the NCLB Title III English Language Acquisition State Grants program. These competitive grants are awarded for up to five years to colleges and universities to provide professional development to improve instruction for English language learners. The remaining $29 million is available to continue professional development projects that were awarded under the 1997 version of the Elementary and Secondary Education Act, before it was reauthorized as NCLB.

Other Programs to Improve Teaching and Learning

The federal government supports several other grant programs for teachers, such as Teaching American History; Math and Science Partnerships; Troops for Teachers; Transition to Teaching; Teach for America; and the American Board for the Certification of Teacher Excellence, among others. The U.S. Department of Education also funds programs to support school leadership, as well as teaching students with disabilities, English language learners, and Native American and migrant children. For more information on grants to improve teacher quality, recruitment and retention teachers should visit: **www.ed.gov/ admins/tchrqual/learn/tpr.**

Report Cards and Parent Notification

Under No Child Left Behind, states and districts must provide the public with information about schools and teachers. Among the required reports are annual state and district report cards and notifications under the "Parents' Right to Know" provisions in the law. These reports will begin with data from the 2002–03 school year.

Report Cards

Essential components that must be included in state report cards are found in Table 2.2.

(*Note:* State report cards may include other information for parents.)

Annual district report cards must report the same information as the state reports, broken down by district level and school level.

TABLE 2.2 • *Annual State Report Cards*

Annual state report cards must include:

- State assessment results by performance level (basic, proficient, advanced), broken out into groups of students by: race, ethnicity, disability status, English language learners, low-income status, gender, and migrant status.

- Accountability information comparing achievement goals and actual performance.

- Percentage of each group of students not tested.

- An additional indicator of student performance, selected by the state, for elementary and middle school academic achievement.

- Graduation rates for secondary school students.

- District and school progress in making Adequate Yearly Progress goals.

- Teacher information:

  Professional qualifications of teachers in the state (degrees, certification).

  Percentage of teachers teaching under emergency or provisional credentials.

  Percentage of classes statewide taught by teachers not meeting the highly qualified teacher requirements, in total and broken out by high-poverty and low-poverty schools.

Source: No Child Left Behind Act.

States and districts must present this information, to the extent that is feasible, in a language that parents can understand, and make it available to the public. For more information on state and district report cards, see the U.S. Department of Education guidance at: **www.ed.gov/programs/titleiparta/ reportcardsguidance.doc.**

National Board Certification

National Board Certification is an integral component of NCLB as it contributes to uniform state standards regarding teacher certification. National Board Certification is a program administered by the National Board for Professional Teaching Standards. Many states have embraced National Board Certification as a major component of their Uniform State Standards Program. National Board Certification results in automatic state certification in a number of states.

National Board Certification is an advanced teaching credential based on teachers meeting rigorous standards regarding specific knowledge and skills that accomplished teachers should possess. It involves a two phase assessment process that covers several months, and a portfolio of instructional materials to demonstrate how a teacher is meeting national board standards. Teachers who are pursuing national board certification must also respond to computer prompts regarding their subject field and certain classroom situations based on national standards developed in their fields. NBC is a voluntary certification program designed to improve teaching practices. National certification is available in twenty four fields listed in Table 2.3.

National Board Certification involves a one-year process where prospective national certified teachers document teaching effectiveness through:

a. Documenting student work
b. Videotaping their teaching
c. Reflecting on their teaching with a view of improving effectiveness

Advanced Certification/Advanced Credentialing

This new, discretionary grant program funds activities that support teachers seeking advanced certification or credentialing. Funds are allocated to high-quality professional teacher enhancement programs that are designed to improve teaching and learning. These advanced certification and credentialing programs assist in identifying teachers who are achieving high levels of instructional quality. These programs are also a tool to

TABLE 2.3 • *National Board Certificates Subject Fields*

- Early Childhood/Generalist
- Middle Childhood/Generalist
- Early Adolescence/Generalist
- Early Adolescence/English Language Arts
- Early Adolescence/Mathematics
- Early Adolescence/Science
- Adolescence and Young Adulthood/Mathematics
- Adolescence and Young Adulthood/Science
- Early Adolescence/Social Studies History
- Adolescence and Young Adulthood/Social Studies History
- Adolescence and Young Adulthood/English Language Arts
- Early and Middle Childhood/Art
- Early Adolescence through Young Adulthood/Art
- Early and Middle Childhood/World Languages Other than English
- Early Adolescence through Young Adulthood/World Languages Other than English
- Early Childhood through Young Adulthood/Library Media
- Early and Middle Childhood/Music
- Early Adolescence through Young Adulthood/Music
- Early and Middle Childhood/Physical Education
- Early Adolescence through Young Adulthood/Physical Education
- Early Adolescence through Young Adulthood/Career and Technical Education
- Early and Middle Childhood/English as a New Language
- Early Adolescence through Young Adulthood/English as a New Language
- Early Childhood through Young Adulthood/Exceptional Needs

Source: The National Education Association.

assist teachers in judging their own instructional performance against a set of high standards, and, thus, they encourage teachers to achieve high levels of performance. A recent study conducted by the National Board for Professional Teaching Standards, which offers advanced certification, sampled a small group of teachers from three cities who had gone through the National Board's certification process. In that sample, a number of teachers had earned National Board status and a number had not. In comparisons between the teachers who became board-certified and those who did not, the board-certified teachers scored higher on dimensions of teaching quality, and in most cases, the differences in scores were statistically significant. National Board-certified teachers also had students who exhibited greater academic skills.

This program provides discretionary grants to state education agencies (SEA); local school districts; the National Board for Professional Teaching Standards, in partnership with a high-need district or an SEA; the National Council on Teacher Quality, in partnership with a high-need district or an SEA; or another recognized certification or credentialing organization, in partnership with a high-need district or an SEA.

This program encourages advanced training of teachers and the connection between teacher standards and student achievement.

State education agencies may apply for grant funds alone, or with a certification or credentialing organization.

How Does NCLB Apply to Students?

Student Improvement

As a provision of the accountability requirement set forth in the law, No Child Left Behind has set the goal of having every child make the grade on state-defined education standards by the end of the 2013–14 school year. To reach that goal, every state has developed benchmarks to measure progress and ensure that every child is learning. States are required to separate (or disaggregate) student achievement data, holding schools accountable for subgroups of students, so that no child falls through the cracks. A school or school district that does not meet the state's definition of "adequate yearly progress" (AYP) for two straight years (school-wide or in any subgroup) is considered to be "in need of improvement."

Accountability for Student Performance

States must develop and implement a single, statewide accountability system that will be effective in ensuring that all districts and schools make adequate yearly progress, and hold accountable those that do not. Schools that do not make adequate yearly progress will be identified for increasingly rigorous sanctions designed to result in meaningful change in instruction and performance. Further, students in low-performing schools will have the option to transfer to other public schools or to obtain supplemental educational services. Finally, the law mandates fundamental restructuring of any school that fails to improve over an extended period of time. Schools are measured on progress they make on an annual basis.

- **Adequate Yearly Progress.** States must establish a definition of adequate yearly progress that each district and school is expected to meet. States must specify annual objectives to measure progress of schools and districts to ensure that all groups of students—including low-income students, students from major racial and ethnic groups, students with disabilities, and students with limited English proficiency—reach proficiency within 12 years. States must set intermediate goals that provide for annual adequate yearly progress targets, with the first increase to occur no later than 2004–05. In order to make adequate yearly progress, schools must test at least 95 percent of their students in each of the above groups.
- **Identification of Schools and Districts in Need of Improvement.** States must annually review the progress of each school and school district receiving Title I funds to determine whether they are making adequate yearly progress, and then publicize and disseminate the results of the review. Title I schools and districts that fail to make adequate yearly progress for two consecutive years must be identified as in need of improvement.

- **Public School Choice.** Students in schools identified for improvement must be provided the option to transfer to another public school that has not been identified for improvement, with transportation provided as based on need.
- **Professional Development.** As previously stated, schools identified for improvement must spend at least 10 percent of their Title I, Part A, funds on professional development for the school's teachers and principal that directly addresses the academic achievement problem that caused the school to be identified for improvement.
- **Supplemental Educational Services.** If a school fails to make adequate yearly progress for a third year, students from low-income families in the school must be provided the option to use Title I funds to obtain supplemental educational services from a public- or private-sector provider, including faith-based organizations, selected from a list of providers approved by the state.

  States must develop and apply objective criteria to potential providers that are based on a demonstrated record of effectiveness in increasing academic proficiency, and must monitor the quality and effectiveness of the services offered by approved providers. States must maintain a list of approved providers across the state, by school district, from which parents may select, and must promote maximum participation by supplemental educational services providers to ensure that parents have as many choices as possible.
- **Funds for Transportation and Supplemental Services.** School districts are required to spend an amount equal to 20 percent of their Title I, Part A, funds to cover supplemental educational services for eligible students and for transportation of students exercising the public school choice option, unless a lesser amount is needed to meet all requests. These funds are not necessarily required to be taken from Title I allocations, but may be provided from other allowable federal, state, local, or private sources.
- **Corrective Action.** If a **school** fails to make adequate yearly progress for a fourth year, the school district must take corrective actions that are designed to promote meaningful change at the school. These corrective actions must include at least one of the following: replacing school staff, imple-

menting a new curriculum (with appropriate professional development), decreasing management authority at the school level, appointing an outside expert to advise the school, extending the school day or year or reorganizing the school internally.

Similarly, if a **school district** fails to make adequate yearly progress for four years, the state must take corrective actions that must include at least one of the following: deferring programmatic funds or reducing administrative funds; implementing a new curriculum (with professional development); replacing personnel; establishing alternative governance arrangements; appointing a receiver or trustee to administer the district in place of the superintendent and school board; or abolishing or restructuring the school district. The state may also authorize students to transfer to higher-performing public schools operated by another school district (with transportation). States must provide information to parents and the public on any corrective action the state takes with school districts.

- **Restructuring.** If a school fails to make adequate yearly progress for a fifth year, the school district must initiate plans to fundamentally restructure the school. This restructuring may include reopening the school as a charter school, replacing all or most of the school staff who are relevant to the failure to make adequate progress, or turning over school operations either to the state or to a private company with a demonstrated record of effectiveness.

- **Technical Assistance.** States and school districts must provide technical assistance to schools identified for school improvement, corrective action, or restructuring. States are required to reserve portions of their Title I funding to benefit schools identified for school improvement, corrective action, and restructuring, and must distribute 95 percent of these reserved funds to school districts. State assistance must include: establishing school support teams; designating and using distinguished teachers and principals who are chosen from schools that have been especially successful in improving academic achievement; and devising additional approaches to providing assistance, such as through institutions of higher education and educational service agencies or other local consortia, and private providers of scientifically based technical assistance.

- **State Report Cards.** States must produce and disseminate annual report cards that provide information on how students are achieving overall as well as information disaggregated by race, ethnicity, gender, English proficiency, migrant status, disability status, and low-income status. The report cards must include relevant information included in Table 2.4.

TABLE 2.4 • *Report Cards*

- State assessment results by performance level, showing two-year trend data for each subject and grade tested, with a comparison between annual objectives and actual performance for each student group. The report cards also must show the percentage of each group of students not tested.

- Graduation rates for secondary school students and any other student achievement indicators that the state chooses.

- Performance of school districts on adequate yearly progress measures, including the number and names of schools identified as in need of improvement.

- Professional qualifications of teachers in the state, including the percentage of teachers teaching with emergency or provisional credentials and the percentage of classes in the state that are not taught by highly qualified teachers, including a comparison between high- and low-poverty schools.

Source: No Child Left Behind Act.

- **School District Report Cards.** School districts also must prepare and disseminate annual report cards that include information on student achievement for the district and for each school. As with the state report cards, achievement data must be disaggregated for the same student subgroups. The report cards also must provide information on the schools identified for improvement.
- **Annual State Report to the Secretary.** States must report annually to the Secretary of Education on their progress in developing and implementing academic assessments; students' achievement on the assessments disaggregated by groups of students; and information about acquisition of English proficiency by children with limited English proficiency, the names of schools identified as in need of improvement, public school choice, supplemental service programs, and teacher quality.

School Dropout Prevention

The Act also includes a school dropout prevention program. This program assists schools with dropout rates above their state average to implement effective dropout prevention and reentry efforts. The program was implemented in response to a national status dropout rate of approximately 11 percent over the past decade (with significantly higher rates in some regions and for some groups of students) and the poor labor market outcomes for those without a high school credential.

The Dropout Prevention Program is essentially a grant program to state education agencies (SEA) and local school districts to implement research-based, sustainable, and coordinated school dropout prevention and reentry programs. At the current appropriation level, grants will be awarded competitively and used for activities such as professional development; reduction in student-teacher ratios; counseling and mentoring for at-risk students; and implementing comprehensive school reform models. The U.S. Department of Education also will create a national recognition program to identify schools implementing comprehensive reforms that have been effective in lowering school dropout rates for all students.

SEAs and districts must implement research-based instructional practices and other activities, and target funds to schools with annual dropout rates above their state average.

Performance Measurement

SEAs and school districts must report dropout data disaggregated by race and ethnicity for schools receiving program funds. State education agencies must:

- Report annually to the U.S. Department of Education on the status of implementation activities and on dropout rates, disaggregated by race and ethnicity, for students at schools assisted by the grant program. In addition, grantees must report annual school dropout rates for the two fiscal years prior to receiving funds under the grant.

Improving Academic Achievement of Disadvantaged Students

The Achievement Gap must be closed for disadvantaged students in reading by:

- **Targeting services to districts that are low-performing and high-poverty.** Eligible school districts are those in each state with the highest numbers or percentages of K–3 students reading below grade level, and include an empowerment or enterprise zone, have a significant number of schools identified for Title I improvement, or have the highest number or percentages of Title I children. States competitively award subgrants to districts, with priority given to districts that have at least 15 percent of students from families with incomes below poverty or at least 6,500 poor children.

Reading First is a formula grant program awarded to states based on the number of children between the ages of 5 to 17 who represent families below the poverty line. States submit an application to the U.S. Department of Education. Grants are awarded based on the recommendation of an expert review panel selected by the Department, the National Institute for Literacy, the National Institute for Child Health and Human Development, and the National Research Council of the National Academy of Sciences. SEAs receiving grant awards will then make competitive grants to eligible school districts. SEAs must make subgrants of sufficient size and scope to enable local districts to improve reading instruction. The amount of the award will be related to each local school district's share of the state's Title I, Part A, funds distributed during the preceding fiscal year, and to the number or percent of K–3 students in the district reading below grade level.

Key Requirements

In addition to developing a process to award competitive subgrants, SEAs must develop a plan on how they will assist districts in using scientifically based reading research to improve reading instruction and raise student achievement. States must provide technical assistance to school districts to assist them in identifying instructional assessments, programs, and materials. States also must develop a statewide professional development strategy to improve instructional practices for reading while ensuring coordination among other literacy programs in the state. In addition, the state must develop strategies for evaluating Reading First.

Reading First will ensure quality by focusing on what works and providing the support needed by SEAs and districts to use the scientifically based reading research to improve reading instruction in kindergarten through third grade. SEAs receiving Reading First grants will support quality by providing professional development that ensures each K–3 teacher will possess the skills necessary to teach scientifically based instructional programs and to use screening, diagnostic, and classroom-based assessments to measure where students are and to monitor their progress. School districts and schools will select instructional programs and materials that support the essential components of reading, leading to a comprehensive reading program. Finally, quality will be achieved as the SEAs and districts provide continuous monitoring and reporting to provide feedback on how well schools, districts, and the state as a whole are progressing toward meeting their goals of having all children reading on grade level by the end of third grade.

Performance Measurement

The goal of the program is to ensure that all children read at or above grade level by the end of third grade. To determine if progress is being made toward the goal, each SEA is required to report annually on the progress of local school districts, including identifying districts that are significantly increasing the number of children who read at or above grade level. Beginning in fiscal year 2004, targeted assistance grants were made available on a competitive basis to SEAs that demonstrate an increase in student achievement related to the Reading First program. At the completion of the third year, SEAs are required to send a midpoint report to the secretary describing their progress toward meeting the goal. There are consequences for not making sufficient progress. The expert panel convened to review state applications will review these progress reports. SEAs that are not making significant progress may lose all or part of the remaining funds or be subject to other actions deemed appropriate by the secretary.

Accountability for Student Programs

NCLB Increases Accountability for Student Performance by:

- **Evaluating the effectiveness of local programs through annual performance reports on their evaluation results.** Local grantees are required to describe how they will evaluate their success in enhancing children's early reading skills. Grantees must report to the U.S. Department of Education annually on their progress and the results of their evaluation.
- **Evaluating the effectiveness of the program through an independent national evaluation.** The new Early Reading First Program is a federally administered discretionary grant program. The U.S. Department of Education will make competitive awards for up to three years to local school districts eligible under statutory criteria for the Reading First program, other public or private organizations within those

eligible districts, or collaborations between both. Eligible Local Education Agencies (LEA) were identified by states, or if not by states, by the Department, and posted on the Department's Web site. These organizations will apply for awards on behalf of one or more preschool programs for the purpose of strengthening the literacy components of existing early childhood centers.

Key Requirements

Grantees must use Early Reading First funds to provide preschool-age children with high-quality oral language and literature-rich environments; provide professional development to staff that is based on scientific research to assist in developing children's language and cognitive skills; identify and provide activities and instructional materials that are grounded in scientifically based reading research; acquire, provide training for, and implement screening reading assessments or other appropriate measures to determine whether preschool-age children are developing the early language and cognitive skills they need for later reading success; and integrate these instructional materials, activities, tools, and measures into the grantee's preschool programs.

In order to prevent reading difficulties for children, Early Reading First programs must focus on skills most related to later reading success and instructional methods and activities that have been scientifically demonstrated to produce learning gains for children in these skills. These programs are required to support children's development of oral language (including vocabulary), phonological awareness (familiarity with individual sounds in words), print awareness, and letter knowledge.

Required activities regarding the Early Reading First program are reflected in Table 2.5.

Performance Measurement

Grantees are required to evaluate the success of their programs in preparing children for school and to report this information annually to the U.S. Department of Education. The law also requires an independent national evaluation of the program. Required evaluation procedures are listed in Table 2.6.

TABLE 2.5 • *Early Reading First Programs*

Early Reading First programs must conduct the following activities that have been shown to be effective in developing the language, cognitive, and early reading skills of young children:

- Provide high-quality oral language and literacy-rich classroom environments.

- Provide professional development to staff that is based on research knowledge of early language and reading development.

- Identify and provide activities and instructional materials based on research to develop children's language, cognitive, and early reading skills.

- Use screening assessments or other appropriate measures to determine whether young children are developing the cognitive skills they need for later reading success.

- Integrate these materials, activities, tools, and measures into preschool programs.

Source: No Child Left Behind Act.

In addition to the specific state requirements, local school districts are expected to meet a number of requirements that the SEA is responsible for monitoring.

Improving Math and Science Instruction Around the Nation

No Child Left Behind also supports the belief that developing teachers' knowledge and skills in math and science will contribute substantially to the goal of improving student learning, and that students will perform better on assessments of math and science if their teachers have in-depth knowledge of the subjects they teach.

In the United States, the professional preparation programs for many teachers at the elementary, middle school, and high

TABLE 2.6 • *Evaluation Procedures for U.S. Department of Education*

State education agencies may:

- Make relevant state standards for reading and language arts available to applicants.

- Identify eligible school districts and develop a process by which to award subgrants to them. The process must clearly describe the selection criteria.

- Develop and implement a statewide program of professional development for teachers, including special education teachers, for kindergarten through grade 3 that will prepare them to teach all of the essential components of reading instruction.

- Provide technical assistance to local districts in selecting and implementing instructional programs and materials based on scientifically based reading research, selecting screening, diagnostic, and classroom based assessment instruments and identifying eligible professional development providers.

- Submit annual reports to the Secretary on the implementation of the program and student achievement outcomes.

- Submit a midpoint report that identifies districts that are making progress to increase the number and percentage of students reading at or above grade level, as well as the statewide progress toward this goal. This interim report is due 60 days after the end of the third year.

- Establish a Reading Leadership Team that will assist in the oversight of the SEAs Reading First program.

Source: No Child Left Behind Act.

---

school levels include very little math and science. Only 43 percent of middle school students take science from teachers who have a major in science and are certified to teach science.

No Child Left Behind requires that federal funds be allocated only to those programs that are backed by evidence of their effectiveness. Over the last decade, researchers have scientifically proven the best ways to teach reading. The same must occur in math. Research-based teaching methods must be used to improve teachers' performance in math.

Student Performance in 2003

Student proficiency in math is presented in Table 2.7. The figures in Table 2.7 indicate that 32 percent of fourth-graders and 29 percent of eighth-graders performed at or above the Proficient level in 2003. The percentages of students performing at or above Basic in 2003 were 77 percent at grade 4 and 68 percent at grade 8.

Math and Science Partnerships

No Child Left Behind creates math and science partnerships to rally every sector of society to work with schools to increase math and science excellence.

The Mathematics and Science Partnership (MSP) program is the signature program for improving math and science education in No Child Left Behind. This program provides funding to every state in the nation on a formula-grant basis to support high-quality professional development for math and science teachers. Each state is required to conduct a competitive grant program to support projects that are partnerships among science, engineering, and mathematics, and other high-tech departments at institutions of higher education, high-need school districts, and other interested organizations, with the purpose of enhancing the content knowledge of math and science teachers. Those interested in competing for funding under this program should contact their district for more information. For more information on the Math and Science Partnership program, teachers should visit: **www.ed.gov/rschstat/research/progs/mathscience/ index.html.**

No Child Left Behind requires states to fill the nation's classrooms with teachers who are qualified to teach math and science by the end of the 2005–06 school year. In areas where

TABLE 2.7 • *Math Proficiency Level 2003*

Thirty-two percent of fourth-graders and 29 percent of eighth-graders met or exceeded the proficient level in 2003, while 77 percent and 68 percent, respectively, performed at or above the basic level.

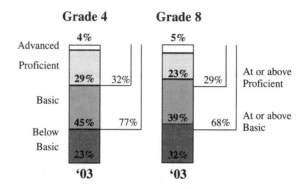

Note: Detail may not sum to totals because of rounding.

Source: U.S. Department of Education, Institute of Education Sciences, National Center for Education Statistics, National Assessment of Educational Progress (NAEP), 2003 Mathematics Assessment.

there are critical shortages, President Bush supports paying math and science teachers increased salaries to attract experienced and excellent teachers. Title II funds may be used to fund programs that attract teachers in areas of critical need.

Table 2.8 presents data regarding student achievement in math and science by race and socio-economic status.

Teacher Liability Protection

The Paul D. Coverdell Teacher Protection Act of 2001 limits the financial liability of teachers, principals, and other school professionals for harm they may cause when acting on behalf of the school in disciplining students or maintaining classroom order. A recent survey of school principals found that 65 percent

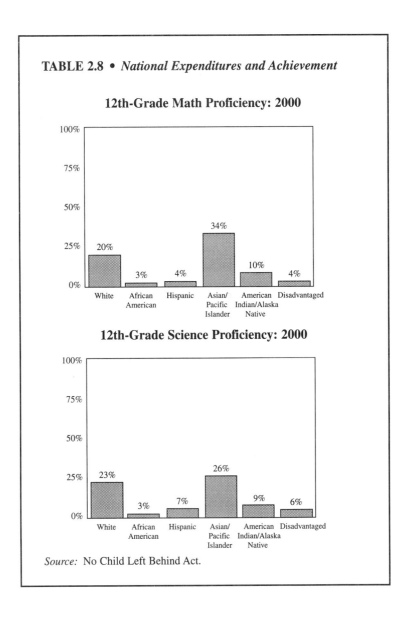

TABLE 2.8 • *National Expenditures and Achievement*

Source: No Child Left Behind Act.

of respondents had modified or, in some cases, eliminated certain school activities due to liability concerns, and a survey of teachers found that liability was among respondents' top three concerns. The new provision will encourage school staff to maintain school discipline and order by removing the fear of being sued for their actions.

This provision protects educators from liability for harm they may cause while disciplining students, and limits the awarding of punitive damages against them, as long as they are acting within the scope of their employment and in accordance with applicable federal, state, and local laws, including civil rights laws. There are a number of exceptions, including violent crimes, sexual offenses, and actions committed under the influence of drugs or alcohol. The law also states that this provision has no effect on any state or local laws, rules, regulations, or policies regarding the use of corporal punishment. The provision applies to teachers, principals, administrators, school board members, educational professionals working in a school, any school employee whose job is to maintain discipline and ensure safety, and any school employee who is acting in an emergency to maintain discipline and ensure safety.

Women's Educational Equity

This program provides financial assistance to enable educational agencies to meet the requirements of Title IX of the Education Amendments of 1972, and promotes educational equity for girls and women who experience multiple forms of discrimination based on gender, race, ethnic origin, limited English proficiency, disability, or age.

The Secretary of Education awards competitive grants to public agencies, private nonprofit agencies, organizations, institutions, student groups, community groups, and individuals. At least two-thirds of the funds are used to award grants that focus on developing model equity programs, and on local implementation of gender-equity policies and practices at all educational levels. In addition, the U.S. Department of Education supports research and development activities that are designed to advance gender equity nationwide and to foster equitable policies and practices in educational agencies and institutions, as well as local communities.

Grants must address all levels of education in all regions of the United States, and in urban, rural, and suburban schools.

The Secretary has the responsibility to ensure that the program is administered within the Department by a recognized professional with qualifications and experience in the field of gender-equity education.

Performance Measurement

The Secretary is to submit to the President and Congress a report on the status of educational equity for girls and women in the United States no later than January 1, 2006. In addition, no later than January 1, 2005, the Secretary is to evaluate and disseminate materials and programs developed under the program, and report to Congress.

Enhancing Education through Technology

Technology can be used to enhance curricula and engage students in learning. In addition, the job market increasingly demands technology skills for new workers. Research has indicated that a digital divide regarding technology access and use exists between students in high-poverty schools and students in other schools. For example, according to the National Center for Education Statistics, in 2000, while the overall ratio of students to instructional computers with Internet access was 7-to-1, in high-poverty schools the ratio was 9-to-1 compared to 6-to-1 in low-poverty schools. Similarly, in 2000, 60 percent of classrooms in high-poverty schools were connected to the Internet compared to 82 percent of classrooms in other schools. Even as technology becomes more ubiquitous in classrooms, teachers' preparation to use technology for teaching lags behind access to technology. In 2000, only 27 percent of teachers reported that they were fully prepared to integrate technology in their instruction. Seventy-seven percent of subgrantees of the Technology Literacy Challenge Fund—the predecessor program to the Educational Technology State Grants Program, which also targeted high-poverty districts—reported that professional development was a primary use of program funds in 2000.

The principal goal of the Educational Technology State Grants Program is to improve student academic achievement through the use of technology in elementary and secondary schools. It is also designed to assist every student in becoming technologically literate by the end of eighth grade and to encourage the effective integration of technology resources and systems with teacher training and professional development to establish research-based instructional models. The program targets funds primarily to school districts that serve concentrations of poor students.

The Educational Technology State Grants Program awards formula grants to states. States may use up to five percent of their Educational Technology State Grants Program funds for state-level activities. States must distribute half of the remaining funds by formula to school districts based on each district's share of funds under Part A of Title I and the other half to high-need districts or partnerships including high-need districts on a competitive basis. Under the Educational Technology State Grants Program, high-need districts are those that (1) are high-poverty and (2) serve at least one low-performing school or have a substantial need for technology.

The program supports improved student academic achievement through the use of technology in schools by supporting high-quality professional development; increased access to technology and the Internet; the integration of technology into curricula; and the use of technology for promoting parental involvement and managing data for informed decision-making. Districts are required to spend 25 percent of the funds they receive on professional development, though a state may exempt a district that demonstrates it already provides high-quality professional development in the integration of technology. In addition, the program will support national activities for disseminating information regarding best practices and providing technical assistance to states and districts and a rigorous, long-term study of the conditions and practices under which educational technology improves teaching and learning.

Key Requirements

SEAs must develop state technology plans that include state goals for the use of technology and the strategies the state will use to prepare teachers to use technology. States also must provide technical assistance in developing applications to high-poverty districts and use accountability measures to evaluate the effectiveness of the Educational Technology State Grants Program. States as well as districts may use program funds to develop performance-measurement systems for tracking their progress. Districts also must develop local long-range strategic educational technology plans to be eligible for formula or competitive grant funding.

The program emphasizes using both proven and innovative strategies for the use of technology. Specifically, the Educational Technology State Grants Program focuses on using technology to support improved curricula, instruction and, ultimately, student achievement by making available the resources necessary for integrating technology into the instructional program. This includes funds for Internet connections and services, professional development for teachers, and technology applications. Districts may participate in the Educational Technology State Grants Program by forming partnerships or consortia with other organizations, other districts, universities, and public-private initiatives that have been effectively using technology or have expertise in applying educational technology in instruction.

Performance Measurement

Participating SEAs and school districts must develop accountability measures for assessing how effective the Educational Technology State Grants Program is in supporting the integration of technology into curricula and instruction, increasing the ability of teachers to teach with technology, and enabling students to meet challenging state standards. In addition, the Department will conduct an independent study to identify the conditions under which technology increases student achievement and teachers' ability to teach with technology improves.

States are responsible for implementing their state technology plans, including tracking progress according to the goals and accountability measures in their plans.

Districts applying for the Educational Technology State Grants Program must describe how they will use Educational Technology State Grants Program funds, including how they will promote the implementation of technology to improve student academic achievement and teacher effectiveness. States must provide technical assistance to high-poverty districts that demonstrate need for assistance in developing applications.

Chapter 3

Parental Empowerment and Innovative Programs

Expanded Parental Options

Under No Child Left Behind, by the 2005–06 school year each state must measure every public school student's progress in reading and math in each of grades 3 through 8 and at least once during grades 10 through 12. By school year 2007–08, assessments in science for grade spans 3–5, 6–8, and 10–12 must be under way. These assessments must be aligned with state academic content and achievement standards. They will provide parents with objective data regarding their child's academic strengths and weaknesses. They will also provide the public with general information regarding the progress of their area schools.

Important Information for Parents on Student Performance

No Child Left Behind requires states and school districts to provide parents detailed report cards on schools and districts, telling them which ones are succeeding and why. Included in the report cards are student achievement data broken out by race, ethnicity, gender, English language proficiency, migrant status, disability status and low-income status, as well as information about the professional qualifications of teachers. With these provisions, NCLB ensures that parents have important, timely information about the schools their children attend.

New Options to Parents Whose Children Attend Schools in Need of Improvement

In the first year in which a school is considered to be in need of improvement, parents receive the option to transfer their child to a higher-performing public school, including a charter school, in the district. Transportation must also be provided to the new school, subject to certain cost limitations. In the second year in which a school is considered to be in need of improvement, the school must continue offering public school choice, and the school must also offer supplemental services (e.g., free tutoring) to low-income students. For more information, teachers should visit the U.S. Department of Education's Web site at: **www.ed. gov/about/offices/list/oii/about/choice.html.**

Expanded Flexibility and Local Control

More Flexible Spending

In exchange for strong accountability, No Child Left Behind provides states and districts more flexibility in the use of their federal education funding. Again, NCLB makes it possible for districts to transfer up to 50 percent of federal formula-grant funds they receive under different parts of the law (Title II— Improving Teacher Quality and Educational Technology, Title IV—Safe and Drug-Free School Grants, Title V—Innovative Programs) to any one of these programs or to the Title I program (Improving the Academic Achievement of the Disadvantaged). This allows districts the opportunity to target resources as they see fit, without any additional approval. As a result, principals and administrators spend less time filling out forms and dealing with federal red tape and devote more time to students' needs. Districts have more freedom to implement innovations and allocate resources, thereby providing local citizens a greater opportunity to affect decisions regarding school programs. The flexibility and transferability provisions for states and districts are described in greater detail on the U.S. Department of Education's Web site at: **www.ed.gov/nclb/freedom/local/flexibility/ index.html.**

Parents' Right to Know

The Parents' Right to Know provision requires that two types of communication be provided to parents of students in Title I schools.

Parent Notification

By District: A district receiving Title I funds must send a notification to parents, informing them of their right to request information on the qualifications of their child's teacher. The information that the district must provide (if requested) includes the following information found in Table 3.1.

By School: Additionally, schools receiving federal Title I Funds must send parents certain information in a timely manner, in a language that is understandable, to the extent that is feasible. Title I schools must provide the following:

- Information on the child's level of achievement on state assessments.
- Timely notice that the child has been assigned to or been taught by a teacher who does not meet the highly qualified teacher requirements for four or more consecutive weeks.

Parental Assistance Information Centers

This program establishes school-linked or school-based parental information and resource centers that provide training,

---

TABLE 3.1 • *Parental Notification by District*

Districts receiving Title I funds must inform parents:

- Whether or not the teacher has met the certification requirements of the state.

- Whether or not the teacher is teaching under an emergency or other provisional status.

- The bachelor's degree major of the teacher and any other graduate certification or degree held by the teacher in the field or discipline of his or her certificate or degree.

- Whether or not the child receives service from a paraprofessional and, if so, his or her qualifications.

Source: No Child Left Behind Act.

information, and support to parents, and to individuals and organizations that work with parents, to implement parental involvement strategies that lead to improvements in student academic achievement.

The research overwhelmingly demonstrates that parent involvement in children's learning is positively related to achievement. Further, the more intensively parents are involved in their children's learning, the more beneficial the achievement is to the child. This holds true for all types of parent involvement in children's learning and for all types and ages of students. Researchers also have found that the schools with the most successful parent involvement programs are those which offer parents a variety of ways to participate.

Provisions Related to Parental Assistance

- The law requires grantees to use at least 30 percent of their awards to establish, expand, or operate Parents as Teachers, Home Instruction Program for Preschool Youngsters, or other early childhood parent education programs. Because parents are their children's first and most influential teachers, these programs train parents in positive parenting skills, and provide the information and support that parents need to provide their child a solid foundation for school success.

Reduced Bureaucracy and Increased Flexibility

- The law authorizes centers to assist schools in meeting the Title I parental involvement requirements, developing school improvement plans, and coordinating family involvement initiatives with less bureaucracy.

Focused Academic Standards

The center assists parents in participating effectively in their children's education so that their children will meet state and local academic standards.

The U.S. Department of Education awards competitive grants to nonprofit organizations and consortia of nonprofit organizations and school districts to establish school-linked or school-based parental information and resource centers. Grants are distributed to all geographic regions of the United States. The first $50 million of the amount appropriated must be used for parent information and resource centers. Any amount above $50 million must be split evenly between the parent information and resource centers and the local family information centers. Organizations must provide required information annually as reflected in Table 3.2.

Key Requirements

Each organization or consortium submits to the Secretary of Education information on the effectiveness of the parental involvement activities that districts and schools are executing that lead to improved student and school academic achievement.

TABLE 3.2 • *Organizations or Consortia Receiving Assistance*

Organizations or consortia receiving assistance under this program report annually on:

- The number of parents who receive information and training, disaggregated by minority and limited English proficient status.
- The types of training, information, and support provided.
- The strategies used to reach and serve parents who are minority, limited English proficient, or have limited literacy skills.
- The parental involvement policies and practices used by the center and an evaluation of whether the policies and practices are effective.
- The effectiveness of the parental involvement activities of districts and schools on student achievement.

Source: No Child Left Behind Act.

Voluntary Public School Choice

According to the 1993 National Household Education Survey, most American families choose their child's school. While 20 percent of parents chose a school other than the public school assigned to their residential neighborhood, an additional 39 percent of families claim they chose their neighborhood for its public school. In effect, 59 percent of American families are making conscious choices regarding schools that best suit their needs. Nearly every state has some type of choice plan, either allowing families to choose a public school within a district, across the state, or among charters or magnet schools. The Voluntary Public School Choice program aids states and local school districts in implementing public school choice policies by providing funds for transportation, tuition transfer payments to the schools that students choose to attend, increasing the capacity of high-demand schools to serve greater numbers of students, and disseminating information about open-enrollment options.

New Features of the No Child Left Behind Act: Improved Accountability for Student Performance

- **The Act requires evaluation of effects.** The U.S. Department of Education will evaluate: (1) the extent to which the programs funded promote educational equity and excellence; (2) the characteristics of participating students; and (3) the effect of the program on the academic achievement of students participating in the program, particularly students who move from low- to higher-performing schools, and on the overall quality of participating schools and districts.

Parental Empowerment

NCLB provides options for parents in low-performing schools. The Act provides a priority for applicants whose program would provide the widest variety of choices and have the greatest impact on students in low-performing schools by providing an education for them in a more rigorous educational setting found in a higher-performing school.

The Voluntary Public School Choice program authorizes competitive awards to state education agencies (SEAs), school districts, or partnerships that include an SEA or a district and another organization. Funding is available to establish or expand programs that provide students and parents with greater public school choice. Grants are extended for five years. Grantees may use up to a maximum of one year for planning or program design.

Key Requirements

States and districts document their public school choice program; how and when parents will be notified of the program; how students will be selected for participation; and how the program will be coordinated with other federal and nonfederal projects. Grantees must provide transportation to participating students. Priority is given to projects that:

- Provide the widest variety of choices to all students in schools participating in the program;
- Have the greatest impact in allowing students in low-performing schools to attend higher-performing schools; and
- Implement an interdistrict public school choice program.

When more students apply than can be accommodated, the plan must select students to participate on the basis of a lottery.

Not only are parents able to choose high-quality programs for their children, but the competition among schools to attract students is designed to result in higher-quality education programs in all schools. In addition, accountability provisions in No Child Left Behind also require that students in low-performing schools have the option of choosing another school that can provide a higher-quality education.

Performance Measurement

The U.S. Department of Education will evaluate whether SEAs have public school choice plans that include: (1) the extent to which programs promote educational equity and excellence; (2) the characteristics of participating students; and (3) the programs' effects on the academic achievement of participating students, particularly those who move from low- to higher-performing schools, and on the overall quality of participating schools and districts.

Key Activities Involving State Education Agencies

State education agencies:

- With approved applications must disseminate information regarding public school choice.
- With approved applications must create and implement program planning and monitoring guidelines for grantees.

Magnet Schools Assistance

The Magnet Schools Assistance Program (MSAP) provides grants to establish and operate magnet schools in school districts that are under a court-ordered or federally approved voluntary desegregation plan to eliminate, reduce, or prevent minority group isolation in elementary and secondary schools. For nearly four decades, magnet schools have been an important element in American public education, offering innovative programs not generally available in local schools and providing opportunities for students to learn in racially diverse environments. A study of 1998 MSAP grantees revealed that the funding provided by MSAP enabled magnet projects to support planning and promotional activities related to their academic programs and services; add specially hired staff to support and enhance school instruction; and provide focused training in program areas or educational methods for teachers and other staff.

Added Features of the No Child Left Behind Act

- **Supports federal technical assistance and dissemination of successful programs.** National activities are expanded to include technical assistance and dissemination activities. Requires the U.S. Department of Education to collect and disseminate information on successful magnet school programs.
- **Builds a grantee's capacity to operate magnet school programs.** The use of funds are expanded to include profes-

sional development in order to build capacity to operate magnet school programs after the grant period has ended.

Reduced Bureaucracy and Increased Flexibility

- **More flexibility is provided in administering magnet school programs.** A district may use its grant to serve students who are not enrolled in the magnet program.
- **Increased flexibility in designing magnet schools.** Enables grantees to use flexibility in designing magnet schools for students in all grades.

Increased Funds for Planning

The cap on the amount of funds that may be used for planning increases from 10 percent to 15 percent in a project's third year.

The Magnet Schools Assistance Program is a discretionary grant program that awards funds to school districts (or consortia of districts) to support magnet schools that are part of an approved desegregation plan and that are designed to attract students from different social, economic, ethnic, and racial backgrounds. An applicant's desegregation plan may be either a required plan (for example, a plan required by a federal court) or a voluntary plan that has been adopted by the applicant and approved by the Secretary of Education as adequate under Title VI of the Civil Rights Act of 1964. Funding priority is given to applicants that demonstrate the greatest need for assistance, propose to carry out new or significantly revised magnet school programs, and propose to select students to attend magnet school programs by methods such as a lottery, rather than through academic examination.

Key Requirements

Districts (or a consortium of local school districts) that receive an award must use it to reduce, eliminate, or prevent minority group isolation, increase student academic achievement, continue the magnet school program after assistance is no longer available, and implement services to improve the academic achievement of all students attending the magnet school program. Grantees also must undertake congressionally specified activities such as employing highly qualified teachers, encouraging greater parental decision-making and involvement, and providing equitable consideration for placement in the program. In their application for program funds, applicants must ensure that they will employ highly qualified teachers, and execute a high-quality education program that will encourage greater parental decision-making and involvement. Furthermore, program funds may be used to employ teachers and acquire books, materials, and equipment. Funds may be spent on supporting activities that are directly related to improving student academic achievement based on the state's challenging academic content standards and student achievement standards or activities that are directly related to improving student reading skills or knowledge of mathematics, science, history, geography, English, foreign languages, art, or music. Funds may be spent on activities to improve vocational, technological, and professional skills.

Partnerships in Character Education

The Partnerships in Character Education program provides grants to design and implement instruction regarding aspects of character such as citizenship, justice, respect, responsibility, trustworthiness, and giving. Character education, especially when it is integral to a school's curriculum and culture and involves collaboration among school staff, parents, and key members of the community, can be effective in improving the school environment.

What's New—The No Child Left Behind Act

- **Requires use of research.** Applicants must provide information that demonstrates that their program has clear objectives that are based on scientifically based research.
- **Supports research.** The U.S. Department of Education may use up to 5 percent of program funds for national activities—including research, development, dissemination, technical assistance, and evaluation, to gather information on effective character education practices and to share that information with grantees.

Reduced Bureaucracy and Increased Flexibility

- **The Act eliminates restrictions on awards.** Eligibility has been extended beyond state education agencies (SEAs), in partnership with districts or nonprofit groups or colleges, to also include districts, which may partner with other districts or nonprofit groups or colleges. Private school children and teachers are authorized to participate. Restrictions on the number of grants that can be made and the total amount of funding each grantee may receive have been lifted.

The Act Eliminates Requirements for State Clearinghouses

Although grantees are no longer required to develop their own clearinghouses, the U.S. Department of Education may establish a national clearinghouse to provide information on model programs and research findings related to character education.

This discretionary grant program authorizes the U.S. Department of Education to award grants to districts, partnerships of states with districts, and partnerships of either districts or states with nonprofit organizations, including colleges. The Department may require grantees to provide matching funds, with a sliding scale based on poverty and the ability to obtain matching funding.

Key Requirements

States and other grantees must implement character education programs that have research-based objectives. In determining the elements of character to include in their programs, grantees may select any elements they deem appropriate, but must consider the views of parents and students in making their selection, and any curricula, materials, and other activities developed under the grant must be secular. Grantees also must link the program with education reform efforts and state content standards.

In addition to requiring that applicants base their programs on research, grantees must conduct comprehensive evaluations of their programs (due at the end of the second year of the grant and no later than one year after the conclusion of the grant period) that address the impact on all students, students with disabilities, teachers, administrators, parents, and others.

Performance Measurement

The law specifies that the following factors may be considered in evaluating the success of grantees' character education programs: discipline issues, student academic achievement, participation in extracurricular activities, parental and community involvement, faculty and administrative involvement, student and staff morale, and improvements in school climate.

Key Activities Involving State Education Agencies

State education agency grantees must:

- Form partnerships with one or more school districts or nonprofit organizations, including colleges.
- Evaluate their programs annually and report their findings to the U.S. Department of Education.

Star Schools

Distance learning can enrich regular classroom instruction and provide high-quality instruction in remote or high-poverty locations where students otherwise do not have access to specialized courses such as advanced placement courses. In addition to providing affordable access to learning opportunities, high-quality distance learning can produce learning gains at least as large as those from traditional instruction.

By 2000, nearly all public schools and 77 percent of their classrooms in the United States had access to the Internet. This ratio has steadily improved. Distance learning is increasingly widespread at all educational levels, including the emergence of "virtual schools" in many states.

The Star Schools program encourages improved instruction in mathematics, science, foreign languages, literacy skills, vocational education, and other subjects. It emphasizes learning opportunities for underserved populations, including the disadvantaged, illiterate, limited English proficient, and individuals with disabilities through the use of telecommunications technologies.

Applications are received from eligible statewide or multi-state entities, which may include a public agency, corporation, or a partnership that includes three or more of the following entities: a school district, a state education agency, an adult and family education program, an institution of higher education, a teacher training center or academy, a public broadcasting entity, or a public or private elementary or secondary school. Funding is provided for such activities as development acquisition, maintenance and operation of telecommunications facilities, development and acquisition of live interactive instructional programming, and technical assistance for the use of such facilities and instructional programming.

Key Requirements

Applicants must propose high-quality plans that provide instruction consistent with state academic content standards or otherwise provide significant and specific assistance to states and districts undertaking systemic education reform.

A five-year grant must not exceed $10 million in any single fiscal year. At least a quarter of the total program funds must be used for instructional programming, and at least 50 percent of the available funds shall be used for the cost of facilities, equipment, teacher training or retraining, technical assistance or programming for districts eligible for Title I Grants to Local Educational Agencies. The federal share is capped at 75 percent for the first and second years, 60 percent for third and fourth years, and 50 percent for the fifth year.

The Secretary of Education may use up to five percent of funds for dissemination, evaluation and other activities that are designed to enhance the quality of distance learning.

Ready to Teach

Teacher preparation and professional development are important to increase student performance. Internet and other telecommunications-based professional development may provide research-based professional development on an ongoing basis to teachers in a variety of locations to help improve teaching and learning. For example, studies of educational technology effectiveness report that teacher expertise in using technology can substantially increase the learning gains associated with using the technology. While 80 percent of public school teachers reported in 1999 that they had access to training in use of the Internet, evaluations report that much of the current professional development is too short and not well integrated with ongoing instruction.

The Ready to Teach program provides grants to a nonprofit telecommunications organization or a partnership of such organizations to carry out national telecommunications-based programming to improve teaching in core curriculum areas. In addition, Digital Educational Programming Grants under this subpart support the development of educational programming that includes student assessment tools to provide feedback on student academic achievement.

The Ready to Teach program provides grants to eligible entities on a competitive basis. The Digital Educational Programming Grants program requires a match of not less than 100 percent of the amount of the grant for three years. In addition, these grants support development of educational programming that includes student assessment tools to provide feedback on student academic achievement, with built-in teacher-support components to ensure that teachers understand and can use the programming for student instruction. Educational programming and materials are required for, or adaptable to, state academic content and achievement standards.

Key Requirements

Grantees will use public broadcasting, the Internet, and school digital networks where available, to deliver video and data in an integrated way. Grantees must train teachers to use materials and learning technologies to achieve challenging state academic content and achievement standards. In addition, grantees must ensure that the project will be conducted in cooperation with appropriate state education agency (SEA), school district, and state or local nonprofit public telecommunications entities. Grantees also must ensure that a significant portion of the benefits available to schools will be available to schools in districts that have a high percentage of children eligible for Title I Grants to Local Educational Agencies.

Performance Measurement

Grantees will prepare and submit to the U.S. Department of Education an annual report that, at a minimum, will describe activities undertaken, including core curriculum areas, the number of teachers using the program in each core curricular area, and the states in which teachers using the program are located.

What's New—The No Child Left Behind Act

- **Clarifies what is prohibited.** The law now clarifies that students must be expelled for possessing a gun in school, not just for bringing a gun to school.
- **Requires that modified expulsions be recorded.** Districts are still able to modify student expulsions on a case-by-case basis, but that modification must now be in writing.
- **Allows certain exceptions.** Exceptions to the expulsion requirement are now expressly allowed in two cases: firearms that are lawfully stored inside a locked vehicle on school property, and firearms that are brought to school or possessed in school for activities approved and authorized by the district, if the district adopts appropriate safeguards to ensure student safety.

This provision requires states to prohibit students from bringing firearms to school or possessing firearms in school, with *school* being defined as any setting under the control and supervision of the district for the purpose of authorized student activities. A definition of *firearm* is provided by reference to another statute and includes not only guns but also other dangerous devices such as bombs, rockets, and grenades. Districts must expel offending students from their regular school for at least one year, although this requirement must be construed in a manner consistent with the Individuals with Disabilities Education Act, and expelled students may be provided with educational services in an alternative setting. Districts may choose to modify these expulsions—in writing—on a case-by-case basis. Districts are also required to refer offending students to the criminal justice or juvenile delinquency system.

58

Gun-Free Requirements

The Gun-Free Schools Act requires each state that receives funds under the Elementary and Secondary Education Act (ESEA), as amended by the No Child Left Behind Act, to have in effect a state law requiring districts to expel for at least one year any student who brings a gun to school or possesses a gun in school. This requirement not only removes potentially dangerous students from the school environment but also provides a deterrent, discouraging other students from bringing firearms to school. Over time, this Act has the potential to create a safer school environment by reducing the number of firearms present in schools.

Overall, 55 states and territories provided information about their implementation of the Gun-Free Schools Act for the 1998-99 school year. These states reported that they expelled a total of 3,523 students for bringing a firearm to school. (One state, however, reported data for total expulsions for all weapons—not just firearms—and therefore the figures reported by this state may overestimate the actual number of expulsions under the Gun-Free Schools Act.) States reported that 44 percent of the students they expelled were referred to an alternative school or placement.

Fifty-seven percent of the expulsions were students in high school, 33 percent were in junior high, and 10 percent were in elementary school. States were requested to report the type of firearm involved, and of these, 59 percent were for bringing a handgun to school, 12 percent were for bringing a rifle or shotgun, and 29 percent were for other types of weapons (such as bombs, grenades, or starter pistols).

States reported that 27 percent of expulsions were shortened to less than one year, and 72 percent of these shortened expulsions were for students who were not considered disabled.

The U.S. Department of Education issues a report annually on the number of expulsions nationally, including changes over time for each state.

- States must have in effect a law that meets the requirements of the Gun-Free Schools Act. State education agencies (SEAs) must require districts to include in their applications for funds under ESEA as amended by the NCLB Act an assurance that they are in compliance with the law.

- SEAs must collect from districts information on any expulsions that are made under the law, and must report that information to the U.S. Department of Education annually, including the name of the school concerned, the number of students expelled from each school, and the type of firearms involved.

Other Major Program Changes

The No Child Left Behind Act of 2001 also included the principles of accountability, choice, and flexibility to work in its reauthorization of other major ESEA programs. For example, the new law combines the Eisenhower Professional Development and Class Size Reduction programs into a new Improving Teacher Quality State Grants program that focuses on using practices grounded in scientifically based research to prepare, train, and recruit high-quality teachers. The new program provides States and LEAs flexibility to select the strategies that best meet their particular needs for improved teaching that will help them raise student achievement in the core academic subjects. In return for this flexibility, LEAs are required to demonstrate annual progress in ensuring that all teachers teaching in core academic subjects within the State are highly qualified.

The NCLB Act also simplified federal support for English language instruction by combining categorical bilingual and immigrant education grants that benefited a small percentage of limited English proficient students in relatively few schools into a state formula program. The new formula program will facilitate the comprehensive planning by states and school districts needed to ensure implementation of programs that benefit all limited English proficient students by helping them learn English and meet the same high academic standards as other students.

Other changes will support state and local efforts to keep schools safe and drug-free, while at the same time ensuring that students—particularly those who have been victims of violent crimes on school grounds—are not trapped in persistently dangerous schools. As proposed in No Child Left Behind, states must allow students who attend a persistently dangerous school, or who are victims of violent crime at school, to transfer to a safe school. States also must report school safety statistics to the public on a school-by-school basis, and LEAs must use Federal Safe and Drug-Free Schools and Communities funding to implement drug and violence prevention programs of demonstrated effectiveness.

Questions Teachers Frequently Ask about No Child Left Behind

NCLB is based on the principles of increased flexibility and local control, stronger accountability for results, expanded options for parents and an emphasis on effective teaching methods scientifically proven to increase student academic achievement.

The No Child Left Behind Act of 2001 (NCLB) amends the Elementary and Secondary Education Act of 1965 (ESEA) by making significant changes in the major federal programs that support schools' efforts to educate all children. NCLB is based on the principles of increased flexibility and local control, stronger accountability for results, expanded options for parents and an emphasis on effective teaching methods scientifically proven to increase student academic achievement.

The following are questions frequently raised regarding No Child Left Behind, specifically as the law applies to teachers. This information will assist teachers in understanding the content and intent of this landmark legislation and how it affects them as they serve in America's classrooms. As states, districts, and schools implement these changes, new questions will arise and new issues will surface. Teachers should also pursue answers from their district and state department of education as the majority of these questions arise from state and district implementation of the law.

Highly Qualified Teacher Requirements

Why Is Teacher Quality Such an Important Issue?

A major objective of No Child Left Behind is to ensure that all students, regardless of race, ethnicity, or income, have the

61

best teachers possible. A well-prepared teacher is vitally important to a child's education.

What Does "Full State Certification" Mean?

Full state certification is determined by the state in accordance with state policy. No Child Left Behind allows states to establish their own certification requirements. NCLB encourages states to develop high standards and to use this opportunity to strengthen and streamline their certification requirements to ensure that talented individuals are not discouraged from becoming teachers, or continuing to teach.

Which Subjects Are Considered the Core Academic Subjects?

No Child Left Behind defines "core academic subjects" to include English, reading or language arts, math, science, foreign languages, civics and government, economics, arts, history, and geography.

What Are the Deadlines for Meeting the Highly Qualified Teacher Requirements?

Beginning with the 2002–03 school year, teachers of core academic subjects who are newly hired to teach in Title I programs must meet all requirements. By the end of the 2005–06 school year, all teachers of core academic subjects must meet the requirements in every state that receives Title I funds. However, teachers who teach multiple subjects in eligible small, rural schools must meet the highly qualified teacher requirements in one subject, but have additional time to meet the requirements in other subjects.

How Do I Become Highly Qualified If I Am a New Teacher?

Those who are considering teaching core academic subjects must meet their state's definition of highly qualified teacher, which includes demonstrating knowledge in their subject area. For this reason, the law requires that new teachers hold a bachelor's degree, have full state certification, and demonstrate subject-matter competency. The teacher may meet this requirement by passing a rigorous subject test in each of the academic subjects he or she teaches. A middle or high school teacher may demonstrate subject-matter competency by having successfully completed, in each of the core academic subjects he or she teaches, an academic major, a graduate degree, coursework equivalent to an undergraduate academic major, or advanced certification or credentialing. New elementary school teachers must demonstrate the required competency by passing a state-approved test.

How Do I Become Highly Qualified If I Am an Experienced Teacher?

Many experienced teachers have already met the highly qualified teacher requirements. Experienced teachers must meet the three basic requirements by the end of the 2005–06 school year. They must have earned a bachelor's degree and full state certification (no emergency certificates). For the third requirement, there are multiple ways for experienced teachers to demonstrate that they have sufficient content knowledge. Teachers may opt for taking a subject-matter test (as determined by the state) or demonstrate competency through the state-developed high, objective, uniform state standard of evaluation (HOUSSE). In addition, middle and high school teachers may demonstrate competency through a major (or its equivalent) or through advanced certification or credentials in the subject they teach. Teachers should contact the state department of education for more information regarding meeting the highly qualified teacher definition in the subjects they teach.

What Are the Basic Requirements in the Federal Law for Highly Qualified Teachers?

The law requires that teachers of core academic subjects meet three basic requirements:

- Hold a bachelor's degree.
- Obtain full state certification, which can be "alternative certification."
- Demonstrate subject-matter competency in the core academic subjects taught.

What Is the High, Objective, Uniform State Standard of Evaluation?

HOUSSE is a system by which the state can determine that an experienced teacher meets the subject-matter competency requirements in the law. Under No Child Left Behind, the criteria for such a system:

- Are set by the state for grade-appropriate academic subject-matter knowledge and teaching skills.
- Are aligned with challenging state academic content standards and student achievement standards and developed in consultation with core content specialists, teachers, principals, and school administrators.
- Provide objective, coherent information regarding the teacher's attainment of core content knowledge in the academic subjects in which a teacher teaches.
- Are applied uniformly to all teachers in the same academic subject and the same grade level throughout the state.
- Take into consideration, but are not based primarily on, the time a teacher has been teaching the academic subject.
- Are made available to the public upon request.

The law clearly recognizes that teachers who have been in the classroom have a variety of experiences and training that may demonstrate their competency in the subjects they teach. Therefore, the HOUSSE system may involve multiple, objective measures of teacher competency. Teachers should contact their state department of education regarding specific HOUSSE procedures.

For teachers who teach multiple subjects, states may develop one streamlined HOUSSE procedure for determining subject-matter competency in multiple subjects, such as in discipline families.

Do Highly Qualified Teacher Requirements Apply to Special Education Teachers?

Yes. If a teacher teaches any core academic subject, No Child Left Behind requires that he or she be highly qualified. However, special educators are not expected to meet the highly qualified teacher requirements if they do not directly instruct students in a core academic subject.

Congress has included the requirements for highly qualified special education teachers as part of the Individuals with Disabilities Education Act (IDEA) reauthorization which was completed in 2004. (See Title 20, Chapter 33 § 1462 of IDEA for more information on highly qualified special education teachers.)

What Activities May Special Education Teachers Carry Out If They Are Not Highly Qualified in the Core Academic Content Areas Being Taught?

Special education teachers often carry out activities that would not, by themselves, require them to be highly qualified in a particular subject. Special educators are not required to demonstrate subject-matter competency in core academic subjects if they do not directly instruct students in those subjects, or if their role is limited to providing highly qualified teachers with consultation on the adaptation of curricula, the use of behavioral supports and interventions, or the selection of appropriate accommodations. In addition, they are not required to meet highly qualified requirements in a subject area if they assist students with study or organizational skills and reinforce instruction that the child has already received from a teacher who is highly qualified in that core subject.

Special educators have critical knowledge that supports teaching and learning, and collaboration is important in order to meet the needs of students with disabilities, in both regular classroom settings and special settings.

Would a Teacher Who Provides Core Academic Instruction to English Language Learners Need to Be Highly Qualified, Even If the Child Already Receives Instruction in the Same Subject from a Teacher Who Is Highly Qualified?

Yes. A teacher of English language learners who provides instruction in core academic subjects needs to meet the requirements, even if he or she is not the only one instructing the students in that subject. However, if the teacher is reinforcing instruction already delivered, or is only providing advisory assistance to a teacher who has delivered the instruction, the highly qualified teacher requirements do not apply.

Can English as a Second Language (ESL) Teachers Demonstrate Subject-Matter Competency in the Subjects They Teach through an Advanced Certificate or Degree in ESL?

An endorsement, degree, or certification in ESL may not be used to demonstrate subject-matter competency, unless the endorsement or certification includes coursework equivalent to that of a subject major, or is in line with other means allowable under No Child Left Behind and required by the state to determine subject-matter competency.

No Child Left Behind requires that ESL teachers demonstrate subject-matter competency in the core subjects they teach. For example, a teacher who teaches math using ESL methodologies would need to demonstrate subject-matter competency in math. A teacher who uses ESL methodologies to teach parts of the general elementary curriculum to fourth-graders must demonstrate competency as an elementary teacher.

In No Child Left Behind, the List of Core Academic Subjects Includes the Arts. What Does the Law Mean by "the Arts"?

While No Child Left Behind includes the arts in its list of core academic subjects, it does not define the term. Each state can determine its own definition of "the arts." For example, some states define the arts to include music, visual arts and dance.

No Child Left Behind does not list biology, chemistry and physics in the list of core academic subjects. Does the law require teachers who teach science to demonstrate competency in each discrete science, or as a general category?

While the list of core academic subjects in the law does not break out the sciences, states must consider their current teacher certification standards and student achievement standards to determine what is an appropriate demonstration of subject-matter competency. If a state currently requires subject-specific certification in the discrete fields of science, then the state may require teachers to demonstrate competency in each discrete field. Alternatively, a state may certify teachers as general science teachers or use other broad categories, such as life sciences and physical sciences. In that case, the state may require new teachers to demonstrate content knowledge through a content exam or major and, for experienced teachers, may develop a high, objective, uniform state standard of evaluation (HOUSSE) procedure, aligned with current certification standards.

What Is Alternative Certification?

It can mean two things. First, alternative certification programs are those that allow candidates to teach while they are meeting state certification requirements. These programs must provide solid professional development for teachers before they enter the classroom and while they are teaching and must also include a mentoring or induction component. Teachers in these programs may teach for up to three years while they earn their state certification, provided that they have met the bachelor's degree and subject-matter competency requirements.

Second, states may create alternate routes to certification. For example, they can adopt a new system supported by the American Board for Certification of Teacher Excellence (ABCTE), which allows teacher candidates to demonstrate their competency through a comprehensive, multi-faceted assessment rather than through coursework in specific education school courses. Teachers who pass the assessment would be considered fully certified before they enter the classroom.

Do Long- and Short-Term Substitute Teachers Need to Meet the Highly Qualified Teacher Requirements?

It is vital that substitutes be able to perform their duties well. Although short-term substitute teachers are not required to meet the highly qualified teacher requirements under No Child Left Behind, it is strongly recommended that a long-term substitute teacher meet the requirements for a highly qualified teacher as defined in the law. In addition, as states and districts establish a definition for "long-term substitute," they should bear in mind that the law requires parent notification if a student has received instruction for four or more consecutive weeks by a teacher who is not highly qualified.

Must Elementary School Subject Specialists Be Highly Qualified in All Subjects or Just the Subject They Teach?

A fully certified, experienced elementary school teacher who teaches only a single subject (e.g., a reading or math specialist) does not necessarily need to demonstrate subject-matter knowledge across the entire elementary curriculum. Rather, such a teacher must pass a rigorous state test in the subject area or demonstrate competency in that subject through the state's high, objective, uniform state standard of evaluation (HOUSSE) procedures.

Conversely, *new* elementary school teachers must pass a rigorous state test in all areas of the elementary school curriculum. As a practical matter, most states are already requiring new teachers, whether generalists or specialists, to pass a general test before they can obtain full state certification. In these states, teachers who choose to pursue subject-area specializations will already have satisfied the requirements for being highly qualified in elementary school.

Specialists in non-core academic subjects (e.g., vocational or physical education teachers) do not have to meet the highly qualified teacher requirements.

May Teachers Teach with an Emergency Certificate or Temporary Permit and Still Be Considered Highly Qualified?

No. New teachers must meet their state's definition of highly qualified in the subjects they are teaching at the time of hire, and full state certification is one of these requirements. Experienced teachers teaching under an emergency certificate or temporary permit have until the end of the 2005–06 school year to earn full state certification. Teachers who are part of an alternative certification program already have earned a bachelor's degree and have demonstrated subject-matter competency. These teachers meet the definition of highly qualified and are given full state certification, under the condition that they will complete certain certification requirements in three years or less.

Do Charter School Teachers Need to Be Highly Qualified?

Yes. All charter school teachers who teach core academic subjects, like other public school teachers, must hold a bachelor's degree and demonstrate competency in the core academic areas in which they teach. They also must have full state certification, unless the state charter school laws specify that such certification is not required for charter school teachers.

For the Purposes of Demonstrating Subject-Matter Competency for Teachers in Middle Grades, Who Determines Whether Middle Grades Are Designated Elementary or Secondary School?

States may determine whether a grade level is elementary or secondary. Therefore, No Child Left Behind does not directly address the issue of whether teachers in middle grades are considered elementary school teachers, with general core content knowledge, or secondary content specialists. For the purposes of determining whether a middle school teacher meets the subject-matter competency requirements of NCLB, states are encouraged to examine, for each core academic subject, the degree of rigor and technicality of the subject matter that a teacher needs to know in relation to the state's content standards and academic achievement standards. The intent of NCLB is to ensure that teachers have sufficient subject-matter knowledge and skills to instruct effectively in the core academic subject they teach.

Is Middle School Certification Allowable under No Child Left Behind?

Yes. The state determines certification requirements.

Are Middle and High School Teachers in Small, Rural Schools Required to Be Highly Qualified in Every Core Academic Subject They Teach?

Yes. All teachers who teach core academic subjects must be highly qualified in each subject they teach.

The Secretary of Education recognizes, however, that small, rural districts face special challenges in ensuring that all of their teachers are highly qualified by the end of the 2005–06 school year. As a result, new teachers who teach multiple subjects in eligible small, rural districts must demonstrate competency in one of the subjects they teach; they may have additional time to do the same in additional subjects. The eligible districts must provide high-quality professional development and a program of intensive support or teacher mentoring for these teachers, as they earn additional subject-matter competencies. Teachers will have three years from their date of hire to demonstrate subject-matter competency in additional subjects, and current teachers in eligible small, rural districts will have until the end of the 2006–07 school year to meet the requirements in every subject they teach. To learn about eligibility of a particular district for this extended time, contact the district or State Department of Education. To find out more about this flexibility, see the secretary of education's letter to the states, available at: **www.ed.gov/ policy/elsec/guid/secletter/040331.html.**

Almost 4,900 districts—or about one-third of all districts nationally—meet the criteria for small, rural districts. There are, however, districts with rural schools that do not meet the eligibility criteria and therefore do not qualify for the flexibility described above. These districts should examine how the resources provided through Title II, Part A, and other federal, state, or local resources can be used to improve and expand professional development opportunities, so that experienced teachers who are not yet highly qualified in the subjects they teach receive high-quality, content-specific professional development and meet the HOUSSE standard for each subject they teach. These teachers may also pass rigorous subject-specific state tests or earn a major or advanced certification.

What Are Other Options for Rural Schools in Need of Teachers Who Meet the Highly Qualified Teacher Requirements in Each Core Subject?

In addition to the professional development that all rural districts offer teachers to assist them in meeting the requirements, districts and schools should consider how distance learning arrangements that enlist the services of highly qualified teachers in other localities can help them meet this goal.

Districts may also hire experts (e.g., scientists, engineers, or artists) to provide content enrichment and practical applications to the content being taught. As long as these experts are reinforcing the regular teacher and not providing direct instruction in the core content areas, they do not have to meet the highly qualified teacher requirements. Some states have made it possible for experts who meet the subject-matter requirements and have a bachelor's degree to earn full state certification through an alternate route.

Adjunct Teacher Corps. As part of his FY 2005 budget, President Bush has proposed an Adjunct Teacher Corps initiative. This initiative would support partnerships between school districts and public or private institutions that would bring well-qualified individuals from business, especially those involving technology, industry, and other areas into secondary schools to teach on an adjunct basis. It would thereby aid in meeting needs in critical shortage areas, such as math and science.

What Are the Requirements in No Child Left Behind for Paraprofessionals or Teachers' Aides?

Paraprofessionals—aides who support services provided in a school—are a valuable resource in any school setting. No Child Left Behind sets clear guidelines for academic qualifications for individuals assisting in instruction in Title I funded schools or classrooms. The law allows teachers' aides to support instruction if they have met certain academic requirements: They must have at least an associate degree or two years of college, or meet a rigorous standard of quality as demonstrated through a formal state or local assessment. Paraprofessionals in Title I schools do not need to meet the requirements if their role does not involve facilitating instruction. For example, paraprofessionals who serve only as hall monitors do not need to meet the same academic requirements. If a person working with special education students does not provide any instructional support (such as one who solely provides personal care services), that person is not considered a paraprofessional and the academic requirements do not apply.

What Is Advanced Certification or Advanced Credentialing?

Advanced certification programs around the nation provide opportunities for teachers to challenge themselves as educators and lifelong students, and to take teaching to a new level as master teachers. In addition, for the purposes of meeting the highly qualified teacher requirements in No Child Left Behind, advanced certification and credentialing are vehicles by which middle and high school teachers may demonstrate subject-matter competency in the subjects they teach. Each state may define these terms and choose how to implement them for the purpose of allowing middle and high school teachers to demonstrate subject-matter competency. To learn more about the different opportunities in your state, contact your state certification or credentialing office.

Accountability

What Is Adequate Yearly Progress? How Does Measuring It Help to Improve Schools?

No Child Left Behind requires each state to define adequate yearly progress (AYP) for school districts and schools, within the parameters set by NCLB. In defining AYP, each state sets the minimum levels of improvement—measurable in terms of student performance—that school districts and schools must achieve within time frames specified in the law. In general, each state begins by setting a starting point that is based on the performance of its lowest-achieving demographic group or of the lowest-achieving schools in the state, whichever is higher. The state then sets the level of student achievement that a school must attain in order to make AYP. Subsequent thresholds must increase at least once every three years, until, at the end of 12 years, all students in the state are achieving at the proficient level on state assessments in reading and language arts, math, and science.

English Language Learners: For newly arrived, first-year English language learners (ELL), states may, but are not required to, include results from the math and, if given, reading and language arts content assessments in adequate yearly progress (AYP) calculations. Either way, students taking both the math and English language proficiency (ELP) assessment would count toward the NCLB requirement that 95 percent of all students participate in the state assessments. Schools and districts may also receive credit for ELL students who have attained English language proficiency as part of the ELL subgroup for up to two additional years after they have become English proficient. This way, schools are not penalized for doing an excellent job helping students become proficient in English. For more information go to **www.ed.gov/nclb/accountability/schools/factsheet-english. html.**

Students with Disabilities: When measuring AYP, states and school districts have the flexibility to count the proficient (passing) scores of students with the most significant cognitive disabilities who take alternate assessments based on alternate achievement standards—as long as the number of those proficient scores does not exceed 1 percent of *all* students in the grades assessed, which amounts to about 9 percent of students with disabilities. (The 1 percent cap is based on current incidence rates of students with the most significant cognitive disabilities, allowing for reasonable local variation in prevalence.) For more information, visit: **www.ed.gov/nclb/freedom/local/specedfactsheet.html.**

Uniform Averaging Procedure: States have the opportunity to determine how many years of data will be used to make an adequate yearly progress (AYP) determination. States may use one, two, or three years of data in calculating AYP. Further, states have the latitude to compare one year of data to two or three years of data in making final AYP determinations. This flexibility enables a state to allow schools the benefit of recent improvements (with one year of data) or limit the effect of poor achievement in one year (with two or three years of data). In addition, states can apply this averaging procedure to their 95 percent testing requirement. For more information, visit: **www.ed.gov/news/pressreleases/2004/03/03292004.html.**

What Happens When a School Does Not Make Adequate Yearly Progress (AYP)?

When a school does not make AYP for two consecutive years, it is identified as in need of improvement. States and districts must provide resources and assistance to support it in making meaningful changes that will improve its performance. Title I funds are set aside by states to use specifically for these schools. No Child Left Behind lays out an action plan and timetable for steps to be taken when a Title I school does not improve, as follows:

- **Second Year:** A Title I school that has not made AYP, as defined by the state, for two consecutive school years will be identified by the district as needing improvement before the beginning of the next school year. School officials will develop a two-year plan to turn around the school. The district will ensure that the school receives needed technical assistance as it develops and implements its improvement plan. Students must be offered the option of transferring to another public school in the district—which may include a public charter school—that has not been identified as needing school improvement.

- **Third Year:** If the school does not make AYP for three years, the school remains in school-improvement status, and the district must continue to offer public school choice to all students. In addition, students from low-income families are eligible to receive supplemental educational services, such as tutoring or remedial classes, from a provider who is approved by the state and selected by parents.
- **Fourth Year:** If the school does not make AYP for four years, the district must implement certain corrective actions to improve the school, such as replacing certain staff or fully implementing a new curriculum, while continuing to offer public school choice for all, as well as supplemental educational services for low-income students.
- **Fifth Year:** If the school does not make AYP for a fifth year, the district must initiate plans for restructuring the school. This may include reopening the school as a charter school, replacing all or most of the school staff, or turning over school operations either to the state or to a private company with a demonstrated record of effectiveness.

Teachers may go to: **www.ed.gov/admins/lead/improve/ sigwebcast.html** to view a webcast on school and district improvement.

How Are Teachers or Schools That Raise Student Achievement Rewarded?

No Child Left Behind requires states to provide state academic achievement awards to schools that close achievement gaps between groups of students or that exceed academic achievement goals. States may also financially reward teachers in schools that receive academic achievement awards. In addition, states must designate as "distinguished" schools that have made the greatest gains in closing the achievement gap or in exceeding achievement goals.

Student Assessment

On Which Subjects Are Students Tested? When Are They Tested?

No Child Left Behind requires that, by the 2005–06 school year, each state measure every child's progress in reading and math in each of grades 3 through 8 and at least once during grades 10 through 12. In the meantime, each state must administer assessments in reading and math at three grade spans (3–5, 6–9, and 10–12). By school year 2007–08, states must also have in place science assessments to be administered at least once during grades 3–5, grades 6–9, and grades 10–12. Further, states must ensure that districts administer tests of English language proficiency—measuring oral language, listening, reading comprehension, reading and writing skills in English—to all English language learners, as of the 2002–03 school year.

Students may still undergo state assessments in other subject areas (e.g., history, geography and writing skills), if and when the state requires it. However, NCLB requires assessments only in the areas of reading or language arts and math, and soon in science.

How Do Annual Assessments Support Teaching and Learning?

It is important to measure a student's progress over time in the subjects taught so that teachers, school leaders, and parents understand how well that student is achieving. Annual assessments allow teachers to compare student progress across time. They allow teachers to determine areas of strength and weakness in student understanding and in their own teaching. They also assist teachers and administrators in evaluating curriculum choices. Annual assessments aid in identifying problem areas for students and provide teachers an idea of specific students that need extra help. A recent Education Trust report entitled *The Real Value of Teachers* affirms the importance of regular student assessment as a means of providing teachers with data to inform them not only regarding a student's progress, but also about their own teaching. Using data from state assessments provides schools a powerful tool to determine the needs of students, so teachers and administrators can work together to develop the appropriate professional development for teachers.

How Are Assessments Handled for Students with Disabilities?

The Individuals with Disabilities Education Act of 1997 requires that all students with disabilities participate in regular assessments to determine if they are meeting the achievement goals set for them under their Individual Education Plans (IEP), as determined by their IEP teams. Alternate assessments are only appropriate when students cannot be assessed through the regular state assessments, even with appropriate accommodations.

Students with Disabilities

Under the direction of the state, schools have the following options for testing students with disabilities:

- Regular state assessment.
- Regular state assessment with accommodations, such as changes in presentation, response, setting and timing.
- Alternate assessment aligned to grade level achievement standards.
- Alternate assessment aligned to alternate achievement standards.

(For more information about accommodations, visit **http:// education.umn.edu/NCEO/OnlinePubs/Policy16.htm.**)

How Are Assessments Handled for English Language Learners?

No Child Left Behind requires that all children be assessed. In order to make AYP, schools must test at least 95 percent of the various subgroups of children, including English language learners. For English language learners who take the regular assessments, states must provide reasonable accommodations. Accommodations may include native-language versions of the assessments. However, in the area of reading and language arts, students who have been in U.S. schools for three consecutive years must be assessed in English, with an additional two years as needed, on a case-by-case basis.

Recognizing that there are small groups of students who are unable to take the reading/language arts assessment because of language barriers, the Secretary of Education provides the following flexibility in determining who is tested: English language learners in their first year of enrollment in U.S. schools have the option of not taking the reading and language arts assessment. These students would take the math assessment, with accommodations as appropriate, and the English language proficiency (ELP) assessment.

Reading

What Do We Know about Teaching Reading Effectively?

Teachers across different states and districts have demonstrated that scientifically based reading instruction can and does work with all children. The key to helping all children learn is to assist teachers in each and every classroom benefit from the relevant research. This can be accomplished by providing professional development for teachers on the use of scientifically based reading programs, by using instructional materials and programs that are also based on sound scientific research, and by ensuring accountability through ongoing assessments. To learn more about National Reading Panel findings, visit **www. nationalreadingpanel.org.**

What Is Being Done to Help Children Learn to Read Well by the End of the Third Grade?

Improving the reading skills of children is a top priority for leaders at all levels of government and business, as well as for parents, teachers, and countless citizens who volunteer at reading programs across the nation. At the national level, No Child Left Behind reflects this concern with the new program called Reading First. This ambitious national initiative is designed to aid every young child in every state become a successful reader. It is based on the expectation that instructional decisions for all students will be guided by the best available research. In recent years, scientific research has provided tremendous insight into exactly how children learn to read and the essential components for effective reading instruction.

Does No Child Left Behind Support Programs to Help Children Build Language and Pre-Reading Skills before They Start Kindergarten?

Yes. The Early Reading First program supports preschool programs that provide a high-quality education to young children, especially those from low-income families. While early childhood programs are important for children's social, emotional and physical development, they are also important for children's early cognitive and language development. Research stresses the importance of early reading skills, including phonemic awareness and vocabulary development. Early Reading First supports programs to help preschoolers improve these skills. These programs can include professional development of staff and the identification and provision of activities and instructional material. Programs must be grounded in scientifically based research, and their success evaluated continuously. For more information on Early Reading, visit: **www.ed.gov/programs/ earlyreading/index.html.**

Scientifically Based Research

What Is Scientifically Based Research?

Scientifically based research is research that involves the application of rigorous, systematic and objective procedures to obtain reliable and valid knowledge relevant to education activities and programs. Because scientifically based research includes different types of research methods, it is critical that the research methods used in a particular study are appropriate for answering the questions that are addressed by the study. Understanding the quality of a research study is critical. Low quality studies of the effectiveness of an intervention or program do not provide trustworthy answers to the question, "Does this intervention or program work?"

How Can Teachers Determine the Effectiveness of an Educational Intervention or Program?

As teachers prepare lessons for their students, they are faced with these questions:

- How do I know what works?
- What intervention is best to support a student who lacks certain skills?
- How do I analyze a program's or intervention's effectiveness?

The field of education includes a vast array of education interventions that claim to improve achievement and be supported by evidence. Practitioners are often faced with the challenge of deciding if the evidence is credible and clear as to whether the practice or intervention is truly effective.

What Works Clearinghouse (WWC). Judging the quality of a research study is not always easy. The Department of Education's WWC provides assessments of the quality of specific studies on the effectiveness of education interventions. The reports indicate whether specific studies provide strong evidence about the effectiveness (or lack thereof) of an education practice. Teachers are encouraged to check the WWC web site periodically. To learn more about the WWC, visit: **http:// whatworks.ed.gov.**

Safe Schools

How Big a Problem Is Crime in Schools Nationwide?

In 2001, students ages 12 through 18 were victims of about 2 million crimes at school, including about 161,000 serious violent crimes (including rape, sexual assault, robbery, and aggravated assault). While overall school crime rates have declined over the last few years, violence, gangs, and drugs are still present, indicating that more work needs to be done.

How Can Schools Be Made Safer?

Title IV of No Child Left Behind provides support for programs to prevent violence in and around schools; to prevent the illegal use of alcohol, drugs, and tobacco by young people; and to foster a safe and drug-free learning environment that supports academic achievement. Most of the funds are awarded to states, which, in turn, award money to districts and community-based organizations for a wide range of drug- and violence-prevention programs. These programs must address local needs as determined by objective data and be grounded in scientifically based prevention activities. They must also involve parents. The effectiveness of these programs must be measured and evaluated continuously.

Learning More: Unanswered Questions Regarding No Child Left Behind

While the U.S. Department of Education strives to provide timely and complete information on No Child Left Behind and how it affects teachers and schools, it is realized that implementation is an ongoing process. As new questions, issues, and ideas surface, more information and guidance may be added. If your questions are not answered in this booklet, please refer to **www.nclb.gov** or call 1-800-USA-LEARN.

Teachers also should contact their State Department of Education or district for more detailed answers to specific questions about state and local requirements and policies regarding highly qualified teachers.

Dispelling the Myths of No Child Left Behind[1]

The No Child Left Behind Act of 2001 (NCLB) has received a great deal of publicity since it became law. For a variety of reasons, from its complexity to misconceptions about it to support for and against it, the law has generated a number of myths. This short list attempts to address the more popular of those myths and report the reality of the law.

---

[1]Based on "Adequate Yearly Progress under NCLB," written by Kati Haycock and Ross Wiener for the National Center on Education and the Economic Policy Forum.

81

Myth: Schools that do not meet annual yearly progress (AYP) goals will be considered to be failing.

Reality: Nothing in NCLB requires states to label any school as failing. The law requires that schools be identified for improvement. Schools that need improvement are not failing. Rather, it means that a school needs to improve in certain areas.

A school that is succeeding in some areas but regularly has problems in others is identified as such—needing improvement. This is not the same as failing. NCLB says that it is not enough for schools to simply get by on averages, as was allowed under the old system.

Educators also have to be concerned with schools where certain groups of students consistently fall short, year after year, and then take specific, meaningful actions to serve those students better.

Myth: Too many schools are making AYP in some states, and too many schools are failing to make AYP in other states.

Reality: Because each state develops its own standards and assessments (and then sets its own cutoff score for what constitutes proficient), the number of schools identified will always differ from state to state.

As each state moves to bring all groups of students to proficiency under a common timetable, such differences should diminish somewhat over time.

Myth: Schools that do not make AYP will be penalized by losing federal funding.

Reality: There are no financial penalties in NCLB for schools that fail to make AYP. In fact, the law requires states to set aside a portion of funds received under the federal Title I program to provide additional assistance to schools that have been identified for improvement. The law restricts how federal funds may be spent in schools on improvement.

NCLB does penalize states that refuse to measure student achievement, hold schools accountable, or help them improve by reducing administrative funds granted to state departments of education. And a state could jeopardize federal funding for its schools and children if it categorically rejects the goals of NCLB by refusing to implement a system of high standards and ongoing improvement for all children. But NCLB does not penalize schools for lack of student achievement.

Myth: AYP means that schools must improve test scores in every single year to avoid being labeled as needing improvement.

Reality: First, it takes two consecutive years of failing to make AYP for a school to be identified as needing to improve. No consequences apply to a school that misses AYP for one year.

Also, AYP stands for adequate yearly progress, not annual yearly progress. If a school makes great gains in one year, only to fall back slightly in the next year, it will still make AYP requirements as long as it stays above the target performance level.

For example, if in a state that specifies 50 percent of its students must be proficient in 2004, a school has 40 percent of students proficient in 2002, improves to 55 percent in 2003 but posts a proficiency level of only 52 percent in 2004, it will not be labeled as needing improvement. Its 52 percent score in 2004 remains above the state target of 50 percent. Also, states may make AYP determinations based on test results averaged over three school years.

Myth: A large number of successful schools will be identified as needing improvement.

Reality: NCLB raises the standard for successful schools. It will make schools and their administrations and patrons take a fresh look at academic performance. Averaged performance among all students, a standard long accepted, will no longer be good enough. Schools considered to be successful based on the average might find themselves labeled as "needing improvement" because groups of their students are not making progress.

83

This is one of the major goals of NCLB: To pull back the curtain that has hidden the consistently stagnant performance of identifiable groups of students. Defining success on the basis of average student progress across student groups has obscured achievement gaps between groups, leaving behind the most vulnerable students.

The Ultimate Reality: The greatest threat to making progress in both raising overall achievement and closing gaps between groups is the belief that low achievement is inevitable because of differences in our society.

Plenty of evidence indicates that America can improve the performance of all students, especially those who have been allowed in the past to slip below average into mediocrity. Our challenge is to make educational excellence the rule.

AYP will tell us a lot about how well our public schools are meeting that challenge. Our response to that information will say a lot about our community's beliefs and commitments.

Emerging Legal Issues Involving No Child Left Behind

The National Education Association (NEA) and school districts in three states have filed a lawsuit against the Bush Administration over the No Child Left Behind Act. They are seeking to free schools from complying with any component of the Act that is not funded by the federal government.

The lawsuit only applies directly to the nine districts listed as plaintiffs in Michigan, Vermont, and Texas. The lawsuit also applies to NEA chapters in the three states listed above plus chapters in Connecticut, Illinois, Indiana, New Hampshire, Ohio, Pennsylvania, and Utah. However, the outcome of this suit may affect school districts throughout the nation.

This lawsuit is consistent with critics of the Act who strongly contend that NCLB is an unfunded mandate that school districts should not be expected to meet without adequate funding. The outcome of this challenge will have significant ramifications for educational reform in America's public schools.

References

Dispelling the Myths of No Child Left Behind, Based on "Adequate yearly progress under NCLB," written by Kati Haycock and Ross Wiener, The Education Trust.

ED Publications, Education Publications Center, U.S. Department of Education, Jessup, MD: The National Education Association.

U.S. Department of Education, Washington, DC, Institute of Education Sciences, National Center for Educational Statistics, National Assessment of Educational Progress (NAEP), 2003 Mathematics Assessment.

86

Index

Accountability for study performance, 26
Adequate yearly progress, 4, 26
Assessment, 5, 76
  Increased freedom, 7
  National Assessment of Educational Progress, 8
  Student, 6
  Teacher, 15

Disadvantaged students, 31
  Academic achievement, 31
  District needs assessment, 20
  Report cards, 21
  School drop-out prevention, 30
  Title II, 19, 20
  Title III, 20

Exceptional students, 5

Gun-Free Act, 59

Limited English speaking students, 5

Magnet schools, 51
  Assistance, 51
  Character education, 53
  Increased funds, 52
  Star schools program, 55
Math and science instruction, 35
Math and science partnerships, 37

No Child Left Behind
  Application to schools, 10
  Application to teachers, 11
  Application to students, 25
  Basic provisions, 1
  Frequently asked questions, 61

No Child Left Behind *(continued)*
 Legal issues, 84
 Major program changes, 60
 Myths, 81–84

Paraprofessionals, 2, 13–14, 72
Parents
 Assistance information centers, 46–47
 Choice, 8
 Empowerment, 3, 49
 New options, 44
 Notification, 21, 46
 Right to know, 45
Public school choice, 4
 Voluntary, 49

Report cards
 At school district level, 21
 At state level, 22
 School drop-out prevention, 30

School improvement, 5
States
 Expanded flexibility and control, 45
 Report cards, 22
 State education agencies, 51
Supplemental services, 4

Teachers
 Advanced certification, 23
 Assistance corps, 18
 Funding for quality, 19
 Improving quality, 19
 Knowledge of subject matter, 15
 Liability protection, 38
 National Board Certification, 23
 New elementary school, 15
 New middle and high school, 15
 Preparation, 11

Proven education methods, 8
Qualifications, 13
Teacher quality Web site, 18
Teaching and learning, 14
Testing, 16

Technology
In education, 41

Unsafe School Choice Option (USCO), 5

Women's Educational Equity, 40